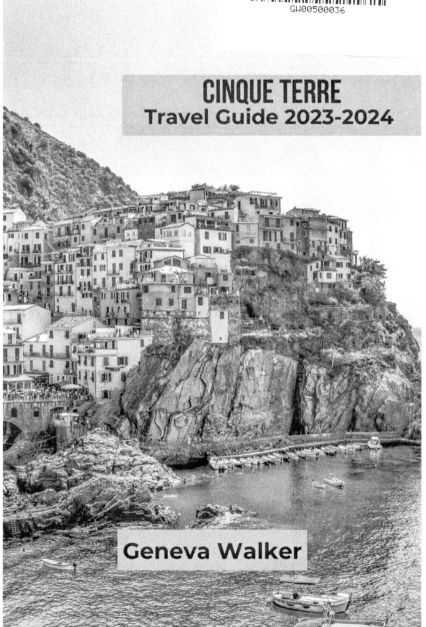

CINQUE TERRE
Travel Guide 2023-2024

Geneva Walker

CONTENTS

INTRODUCTION

About Cinque Terre

Cinque Terre is a territory in the Liguria province of Italy, on the western coast of the nation. It comprises of five villages: Monterosso al Mare, Vernazza, Corniglia, Manarola, and Riomaggiore. The term Cinque Terre means "five lands" in Italian, and alludes to the harsh and rocky terrain that divides the communities from each other and the rest of the world.

The history of Cinque Terre extends back to the Middle Ages when the settlements were created as fishing and agricultural communities. The residents erected terraces on the steep hillsides to raise grapes, olives, and other crops. They also erected stone walls and castles to protect themselves against pirates and intruders. The remoteness of Cinque Terre preserves its distinct culture and customs, as well as its architectural and natural beauties.

In 1997, Cinque Terre was proclaimed a Unesco World Heritage Site, recognizing its extraordinary importance as a cultural landscape. It is both a national park and a marine protected area, trying to maintain its biodiversity and ecosystem. Cinque Terre draws millions of tourists every year, who come to appreciate its colorful buildings, breathtaking vistas, and lovely ambiance. It is also a popular site for hiking, swimming, boating, and wine tasting.

However, Cinque Terre is not without obstacles. The rising tourist demand, the environmental hazards, and the social changes pose challenges to its viability and authenticity. The local authorities and people are working together to create solutions that balance the demands of conservation and development while honoring the uniqueness and tradition of Cinque Terre.

In this book, you will discover all you need to know to organize your vacation to Cinque Terre. You will learn about the best methods to travel there, where to stay, what to see and do, and how to appreciate the local food and culture. You will also find some tips and methods to escape the crowds and make the most of your stay in this wonderful place.

Cinque Terre: A Journey of Discovery and Friendship

I never intended to visit Cinque Terre. It was a spur-of-the-moment decision, a random pick among several probable places in Italy. But as soon as I arrived in this magnificent place, I knew I had made the proper decision. Cinque Terre is a cluster of five lovely towns, nestled among some of the most stunning coastline scenery in the world. Each town has its beauty and character, and together they constitute a Unesco World Heritage Site that draws millions of people every year.

But Cinque Terre is much more than simply a postcard-perfect getaway. It is also a location where you can meet great people, learn about the local culture and history, and enjoy the basic joys of life.

During my visit, I had the chance to explore each hamlet with the aid of pleasant and expert tour guides, who showed me the ideal areas to appreciate the views, enjoy the excellent food, and feel the unique ambiance. I also met other travelers from other nations and backgrounds, who shared my enthusiasm for adventure and exploration. We immediately became friends, and together we went along the magnificent paths that link the towns, swam in the pure blue waters of the Mediterranean Sea, and watched the sunsets that painted the sky in spectacular hues.

In this travel guide, I will share with you my tales and recommendations on how to make the most of your vacation to Cinque Terre. You will discover thorough information on how to get there, where to stay, what to see and do, and how to escape the crowds and enjoy the hidden jewels. You will also explore the history and culture of this unique area, and how its people have retained their traditions and identity despite the difficulties of modernity. Whether you are seeking a tranquil retreat, a cultural immersion, or an energetic adventure, Cinque Terre offers something for everyone. And who knows, maybe you may even discover some new pals along the road.

History of Cinque Terre

The term Cinque Terre, meaning "Five Lands", dates back to before the 15th century, but the history of this fascinating area stretches far deeper. The first human settlements in the area can be traced to prehistoric times, as evidenced by bones and primitive tools found in caves and grottos. The Ligurian tribes who inhabited the shore were subsequently captured by the Romans, who left behind evidence of their presence in villas, highways, and fortresses.

The Middle Ages saw the rise of the Republic of Genoa, a powerful maritime state that dominated the Ligurian Sea and its trade routes. The Cinque Terre settlements were part of Genoa's jurisdiction and enjoyed its protection and privileges. The residents constructed terraces on the steep slopes to produce grapes and olives, producing a distinctive environment that still distinguishes the area today. They also fortified their communities with castles, towers, and walls to protect themselves against pirate invasions and competing forces.

The Cinque Terre endured a period of deterioration from the 17th to the 19th century, owing to wars, plagues, famines, and landslides. Many individuals moved to other nations in pursuit of better prospects. The area remained isolated and impoverished until the development of the railway line between Genoa and La Spezia in the 1870s, which opened up new opportunities for contact and trade. However, it also brought about changes in the traditional way of life and culture of the inhabitants.

The 20th century saw the expansion of tourism in Cinque Terre, as more and more people were drawn by its natural beauty, cultural history, and real charm. The territory became a national park in 1999 and a UNESCO World Heritage Site in 1997, in recognition of its remarkable importance and uniqueness. The Cinque Terre has suffered certain obstacles and risks, including mass tourism, environmental deterioration, and natural calamities. In 2011, a massive flood and mudslide devastated Vernazza and Monterosso, inflicting major damage and fatalities.

Today, Cinque Terre is one of the most popular destinations in Italy and the world, attracting millions of tourists every year. The locals strive to preserve their identity and traditions while adapting to modern demands and opportunities. They continue to produce high-quality products such as wine, olive oil, pesto, and anchovies, using ancient techniques and methods. They also engage in many festivals and events that highlight their history and culture, such as the Festa del Mare (Feast of the Sea), the Festa dei Limoni (Lemon Festival), and the Festa di San Lorenzo (Feast of Saint Lawrence).

Cinque Terre is a location where history meets nature, where tradition meets innovation, and simplicity meets beauty. It is a location that will fascinate you with its colors, tastes, noises, and tales. It is a destination that will make you fall in love with Italy.

Geography

Cinque Terre is a gorgeous location in the Liguria region of northwest Italy, on the shore of the Ligurian Sea. The name means "five lands" and alludes to the five magnificent settlements that cling to the rocky cliffs along the coast: Monterosso al Mare, Vernazza, Corniglia, Manarola, and Riomaggiore. The communities are linked by a network of hiking routes, a railway line, and a ferry service. The region spans an area of roughly 18 square kilometers (7 square miles) and has a population of around 4,000.

The area is defined by its steep and rough landscape, which has been formed by millennia of human activity and environmental erosion. The settlements are constructed on terraces that slope down to the sea, providing a harmonic contrast between the colorful buildings and the turquoise ocean. The environment is also lined with vineyards, olive groves, lemon orchards, and pine woods, which generate some of the region's specialties, such as Sciacchetrà wine, pesto sauce, and limoncello liqueur.

The region is part of the Cinque Terre National Park, which was formed in 1999 to safeguard the natural and cultural legacy of the area. The park is also a UNESCO World Heritage Site since 1997 since it provides an exceptional example of a Mediterranean environment that has been modified by human interaction with nature over generations. The park provides a range of activities and attractions for tourists, such as hiking, biking, kayaking, snorkeling, and sightseeing.

Cinque Terre is a unique and intriguing place for those who wish to enjoy the beauty and charm of the Italian Riviera. The area provides a blend of history, culture, and wildlife that will capture your senses and stimulate your creativity. Whether you are searching for romance, adventure, or leisure, you will find it at Cinque Terre.

CHAPTER 1

PLANNING YOUR TRIP TO CINQUE TERRE

Cinque Terre is a dream destination for many people, with its colorful towns, craggy cliffs, and sparkling water. Whether you're searching for a romantic holiday, a cultural immersion, or an energetic adventure, you'll find lots of alternatives to fit your interests and budget.

The area is a UNESCO World Heritage Site that maintains the beauty and traditions of the Ligurian coast, with its terraced vineyards, old pathways, and local gastronomy. Cinque Terre is a site for those who are searching for a genuine, distinctive, and memorable experience.

In this chapter, we will give you suggestions and information on how to arrange your vacation to Cinque Terre. From selecting the ideal time to visit to locating the greatest places to stay and the top things to see, we will cover all the crucial information you need to make your trip successful.

Whether you are going alone or with your loved ones, read on as we show you how to organize your perfect vacation to Cinque Terre.

When to Go to Cinque Terre

Cinque Terre is a year-round attraction, but each season has its benefits and downsides. Depending on your interests and goals, you may wish to select the optimum time to visit this magnificent location. Here are some elements to consider while organizing your trip:

Weather

Cinque Terre boasts a temperate Mediterranean environment, with pleasant summers and chilly winters. The average temperature varies from 38°F (3°C) in January to 83°F (28°C) in July and August. The water temperature is similarly good, reaching 77°F (25°C) in August.

However, Cinque Terre is also prone to rain, particularly in autumn and winter. The wettest month is October, with an average of 6 inches (152 mm) of rain. The driest month is July, with less than 1 inch (25 mm) of rain.

Rain might hamper your hiking plans, since certain paths may be restricted or treacherous owing to mudslides or erosion. It may also cause floods and damage to the communities and infrastructure. Therefore, it is essential to verify the weather forecast and trail conditions before you travel.

Crowds

Cinque Terre is an extremely famous tourist attraction, drawing millions of people every year. The peak season is summer, from June through August, when the weather is bright and pleasant, and the towns are bustling and colorful. However, this also means that the trails, beaches, trains, and lodgings are busy and pricey. You may have to cope with lengthy lines, restricted availability, and diminished quality of service.

The low season is winter, from November to February, when the weather is cold and wet, and the villages are quiet and serene. This is the perfect time to escape the crowds and experience the unique environment of Cinque Terre. However, this also implies that certain hotels, restaurants, and attractions may be closed or have restricted hours. You may also miss some of the activities and festivals that take place in other seasons.

The shoulder seasons are spring and autumn, from March to May, and from September to October, when the weather is nice and changeable, and the villages are fairly busy and lovely. This is a fantastic time to experience the best of both worlds: comfortable temps, fewer visitors, cheaper pricing, and more availability. However, you may also face occasional wet days or trail closures.

Events

Cinque Terre holds various events and festivals throughout the year, highlighting its culture, history, and customs. Some of the more prominent ones are:

- **Sciacchetrail:** A trail running event that takes place in March or April, along the pathways of Cinque Terre. The event blends sport, nature, and wine culture, as competitors may sample the local Sciacchetrà wine at the refreshment spots.

- **Festa del Mare:** A sea celebration that takes place in June or July in Monterosso al Mare. The celebration comprises a parade of boats decked with flowers and lights, followed by fireworks and music.

- **Festa di San Lorenzo:** A patron saint celebration that takes place on August 10th in Manarola. The celebration involves a religious service, a street market, music, and a fire display.

- **Festa dell'Uva:** A grape festival that takes place in September or October in Vernazza. The event commemorates the harvest of the grapes needed to manufacture Sciacchetrà wine. The celebration comprises a procession of floats symbolizing the several phases of wine production, followed by wine sampling and dancing.

- **Presepe Vivente:** A live nativity scene that takes place on December 24th in Riomaggiore. The tableau recreates the birth of Jesus Christ in a cave near the town, with local people costumed as biblical figures.

Our Recommendations

Based on the criteria described above, we suggest visiting Cinque Terre in May or September. These two months provide the ideal balance between weather, people, and events. You may enjoy the bright and pleasant days, the blossoming flowers or the changing colors of the leaves, the reasonable number of travelers, and the reduced rates. You may also join in some of the events and festivals that take place in these months, such as Sciacchetrail or Festa dell'Uva.

However, if you don't mind the cold and rain, or if you want a more serene and genuine experience, you may also visit Cinque Terre in winter. You may have the trails and towns virtually to yourself, and enjoy the pleasant ambiance of the local cafés and eateries. You may also experience some of the Christmas customs, such as Presepe Vivente or the lighting of Manarola.

We do not suggest visiting Cinque Terre in summer unless you are willing to cope with the heat, humidity, crowds, and expensive pricing. You may also encounter some difficulty in locating lodging or transportation, as well as certain limitations on access to the trails or beaches. However, if you decide to visit Cinque Terre in the summer, you may still have a terrific experience if you plan properly, book in advance, and avoid busy hours.

Whatever time of year you choose to visit Cinque Terre, you will undoubtedly fall in love with this wonderful location. Cinque Terre is a destination that provides something for everyone, whether you are searching for nature, culture, or adventure. It is a location that will inspire you, amaze you, and make you want to come back again and again.

How to travel to Cinque Terre

Cinque Terre is situated in the Liguria area of Italy, between Genoa and La Spezia. There are numerous ways to visit this gorgeous area, depending on your money, time, and tastes. Here are some of the most prevalent options:

- By train: This is the quickest and fastest method to arrive at Cinque Terre since the railway line links all five towns and goes down the coast. You may take a train from any large city in Italy, such as Rome, Milan, Florence, or Venice, then change to La Spezia or Genoa for a local train to Cinque Terre. The travel duration varies based on the number of stops and connections, but it normally takes between 3 and 5 hours from Rome, 2 and 4 hours from Milan, 2 and 3 hours from Florence, and 4 and 6 hours from Venice.

The train tickets cost between 20 and 50 euros one way, depending on the kind of train and the season. You may purchase tickets online or at the station, but it is best to reserve in advance, particularly during busy months. You may also acquire a Cinque Terre Card, which offers you unrestricted access to the trains and buses inside the national park, as well as discounts on select activities and services. The card costs 16 euros per day or 29 euros for two days.

- **By car:** Driving to Cinque Terre is not advised, since the roads are small, twisting and sometimes crowded. Parking is also highly restricted and costly in the villages, and some of them are blocked by vehicles. However, if you want to go by vehicle, you may park in La Spezia or Levanto and take a train or a boat to Cinque Terre. Alternatively, you may park at one of the approved sites outside the villages and walk or take a shuttle bus to the center. The parking prices vary based on the location and the season, but they normally run from 10 to 25 euros per day. You may also get a Cinque Terre Card with parking included, which costs 29 euros per day or 42 euros for two days.

- **By boat:** Another picturesque method to reach Cinque Terre is by boat since you can enjoy the views of the coast and the towns from the water. Various businesses provide boat trips or ferry services from

La Spezia, Portovenere, Lerici, or Levanto to Cinque Terre. The boat rides take between 15 minutes and an hour, depending on the launch location and the destination. The boat tickets cost between 10 and 20 euros for one trip or between 20 and 35 euros for a day pass. You may purchase them online or at the port, but it is essential to verify the weather conditions and the schedule before you arrive, since the boats may not run in case of terrible weather or low demand.

- **By plane:** The closest airports to Cinque Terre are Genoa Cristoforo Colombo Airport (GOA) and Pisa Galileo Galilei Airport (PSA), both roughly 100 km apart from La Spezia. You may travel to these airports from numerous European cities, such as London, Paris, Berlin, or Barcelona, with different airlines, such as Ryanair, EasyJet, or Alitalia. The airplane tickets cost between 50 and 200 euros one way, depending on the carrier and the season. You may then take a bus or a cab to the railway station and get a train to Cinque Terre. The bus tickets cost between 5 and 10 euros one trip while the cab costs vary from 80 to 150 euros one way.

- **By bus:** There are no direct buses to Cinque Terre from other cities in Italy or Europe, but you may take a bus to La Spezia or Genoa and then take a train or a boat to Cinque Terre. Various bus companies provide long-distance trips throughout Italy and Europe, such as Flixbus, Eurolines or Baltour. The bus tickets cost between 10 and 40 euros one way, depending on the distance and the season. You may purchase them online or at the bus terminal.

There are several routes to go to Cinque Terre, each with its pros and cons. You may select the one that fits you best according to your choices and demands. Whatever you chose, you will be rewarded with a memorable experience in one of the most beautiful spots in Italy.

Getting Around Cinque Terre

Cinque Terre is a gorgeous location in northern Italy, noted for its five lovely towns nestled on the craggy coastline of the Ligurian Sea. If you are intending to visit this UNESCO World Heritage Site, you may wonder how to travel about and experience its magnificence. Here are some recommendations and possibilities for you to pick from.

By Train

The train is the most convenient and cheap means of getting between the five towns of Cinque Terre: Riomaggiore, Manarola, Corniglia, Vernazza, and Monterosso. Every hamlet has a railway station and trains operate regularly along the coast, particularly during the peak season from March to November. You may purchase single tickets or choose the Cinque Terre Card, which offers unlimited train travel on the Levanto - Cinque Terre - La Spezia route, as well as access to hiking trails, museums, and wi-fi hotspots. You can get more information about the card and the train itinerary on the official website of Cinque Terre National Park.

By Hiking

Hiking is one of the greatest ways to appreciate the natural beauty and charm of the Cinque Terre. Various routes link the settlements, affording spectacular views of the sea, the vineyards, and the colorful buildings. The most renowned and simplest one is the Blue Path (Sentiero Azzurro), which hugs the shoreline and can be completed in approximately 5 hours. However, certain portions of this path may be blocked due to maintenance or landslides, so be sure to check the status before you start your trip. You may also explore additional routes that head up to the hills or surrounding sanctuaries, but be prepared for more hard terrain and elevation variations. To access most of the trails, you need to obtain the Cinque Terre Card or pay a nominal charge at the gate. You can discover more information about the trails and their difficulties on this website.

By Boat

The boat is another great option to admire Cinque Terre from a different perspective. You can hop on and off the ferries that run between four of the five villages (Corniglia is not accessible by boat) and also to other nearby destinations such as Portovenere, Lerici, and La Spezia. The boat service runs from late March to early November, depending on weather conditions. You may purchase single tickets or a day pass that permits you to go unlimitedly on the boats. You may discover more information about the boat schedule and rates on this website.

By Bus

The bus is not a frequent mode of traveling through Cinque Terre, since no buses are operating between the villages. However, each hamlet has its local bus service that links the lower portion of the town with the higher section or with neighboring attractions. For example, you may take a bus from Riomaggiore to its sanctuary, from Manarola to Volastra, from Corniglia to its railway station or beach, from Vernazza to its sanctuary, or from Monterosso to Levanto. The buses are electric and eco-friendly, and they are included in the Cinque Terre Card. You may discover more information about the bus routes and timetables on this website: https://cinqueterre-travel.com/getting_there/bus/

To summarise, Cinque Terre is a destination that gives various possibilities for traveling about and appreciating its beauty. Whether you want to travel by rail, hiking, boat, or bus, you will find something that meets your taste and budget. Just remember to verify the availability and conditions of each form of transport before you travel, and to respect the environment and the local culture. Cinque Terre is a gem that ought to be maintained and enjoyed.

Choosing the Best Accommodations

Cinque Terre is a gorgeous area of Italy, where five lovely towns cling to the rough coastline of the Ligurian Sea. Each hamlet has its charm and character and provides a selection of lodgings to suit varied preferences and budgets. Whether you choose a comfortable bed & breakfast, a trendy hotel, or a self-catering apartment, you may find the right location to stay in Cinque Terre.

Bed and Breakfasts

If you want to experience the local warmth and culture, a bed and breakfast can be the best option for you. Bed and breakfasts are mainly family-run enterprises, where you may enjoy a warm greeting, a comfortable room, and a tasty breakfast. Bed & breakfasts are notably widespread in Monterosso, the biggest and most accessible of the five communities. Some of them provide sea views, balconies, or patios, where you may rest and observe the surroundings.

Millstone House

This beautiful bed & breakfast is situated in La Spezia, a 5-minute walk from the railway station that links you to the Cinque Terre settlements. It provides contemporary and large rooms with free Wi-Fi, air conditioning, flat-screen TV, kettle, fridge, and private bathroom. Some rooms additionally offer a garden view or a patio. The bed and breakfast offers a garden, a patio, and a bar, where you may have a drink or a snack.

Real Rooms

This elegant bed & breakfast is situated in La Spezia, near the railway station and the ferry port that connect you to the Cinque Terre settlements. It provides pleasant and sophisticated rooms with free Wi-Fi, air conditioning, flat-screen TV, kettle, fridge, and private bathroom. Some rooms additionally feature a balcony or a city view. The bed and breakfast includes a baggage storage facility and a pleasant staff who can aid you with suggestions and information.

Scorci Di Mare

This old bed & breakfast is situated in Riomaggiore, one of the Cinque Terre communities. It provides sea-view rooms with free Wi-Fi, satellite TV, tea, a fridge, and a private bathroom. Some rooms additionally feature a balcony or a kitchenette. The bed and breakfast is housed in a 14th-century structure that has been refurbished using eco-friendly materials.

Hotels

If you like to have additional facilities and services in your lodging, you may select from several hotels in Cinque Terre. These houses vary from budget-friendly to opulent, and from oceanfront to hilltop. You can select the one that suits your style and demands.

Hotel La Colonna

This upmarket hotel is situated in Monterosso, the biggest and most accessible of the Cinque Terre settlements. It provides big apartments with balconies or patios facing the beach or the garden. The hotel contains a saltwater pool with cabanas and loungers, a spa that gives massages and facials, a fitness center that offers yoga and pilates classes, and a kids' club that offers games and crafts. The hotel includes two restaurants that serve Caribbean and Mediterranean food and two bars that provide beverages and live music.

Hotel La Vigna

This boutique hotel is situated in Moneglia, a lovely hamlet on the Ligurian coast, near the Cinque Terre settlements. It provides beautiful accommodations with balconies or patios overlooking the sea or vineyards. The hotel features an outdoor pool with loungers and umbrellas, a tennis court with racquets and balls, and a fitness center with treadmills and weights. The hotel provides free Wi-Fi, cable TV, DVD player, and iPod dock in each room, plus complimentary beach chairs, umbrellas, towels, and coolers on the beach.

Bohio Dive Resort

This diving resort is situated on Grand Turk Island, a tiny island in the Turks and Caicos archipelago, near the Cinque Terre towns. It provides basic rooms with balconies or patios facing the beach or the garden. The diving resort contains an outdoor pool with loungers and umbrellas, a dive store that provides equipment rental and dive tours, and a gift shop that sells souvenirs and supplies. The diving resort features one restaurant that provides Caribbean and international cuisine and one bar that offers beverages and live music.

Villas and Rentals

If you wish to have more solitude and room during your stay, you may select from several villas and rentals in Cinque Terre. These homes vary from flats to mansions, ranging from seaside to hilltop. You can select the one that meets your budget and desire.

Villa Renaissance

This home is situated in Monterosso, the biggest and most accessible of the Cinque Terre settlements. It provides luxury rooms with balconies or patios facing the ocean or the pool. The villa offers a heated pool with a jacuzzi and a swim-up bar, a tennis court with racquets and balls, and a fitness center with treadmills and weights. The villa includes free Wi-Fi, cable TV, a DVD player, and an iPod dock in each room, plus complimentary beach chairs, umbrellas, towels, and coolers on the beach.

The Shore Club

This home is situated on Long Bay Beach, a lovely beach on the Turks and Caicos island of Providenciales, near the Cinque Terre communities. It provides magnificent homes with private pools and balconies overlooking the ocean. The property contains a main pool with cabanas and daybeds, a lap pool with a waterfall and a bridge, and a spa pool with a sauna and a steam room. The villa also contains a spa that gives massages and body treatments, a fitness facility that offers personal trainers and courses, and a kids' club that offers activities and childcare. The villa offers three restaurants that serve Asian, Italian, and local food, and two bars that provide beverages and snacks.

Whitby Beach House

This beach home is situated on Whitby Beach, a magnificent beach on the Turks and Caicos island of North Caicos, near the Cinque Terre settlements. It provides pleasant rooms with ceiling fans, mosquito nets, and private bathrooms. The beach house offers a big deck with hammocks, seats, and tables, a grilling area with a grill and a sink, and a gazebo with a swing and a view of the ocean. The beach house provides free Wi-Fi, literature, games, and puzzles in the common area, plus complimentary bikes, kayaks, snorkeling gear, and fishing rods for guests to use.

Locanda Il Carugio

This inn is situated in Corniglia, one of the Cinque Terre settlements. It provides stylish rooms with free Wi-Fi, air conditioning, flat-screen TV, kettle, fridge, and private bathroom. Some rooms additionally offer a garden view or a patio. The inn features a garden, a patio, and a communal lounge, where you may relax and chat with other guests.

Hostels

If you are seeking budget-friendly and sociable lodging, you may select from a few hostels in Cinque Terre. These establishments provide dormitory-style rooms with common toilets, and occasionally individual rooms as well. Hostels are a terrific way to meet other travelers and frequently feature common spaces, kitchens, and activities.

5 Terre Backpackers

This hostel is situated in Corvara, a tiny town outside the Cinque Terre National Park. It provides mixed and female-only dormitories with free Wi-Fi, lockers, and bedding. The hostel features a garden, a patio, and a lounge, where you can enjoy the views of the mountains and the sea. The hostel also provides free breakfast, free shuttle service to the railway station, and free guided hikes.

Mar-Mar

This hostel is situated in Riomaggiore, one of the Cinque Terre settlements. It provides mixed dormitories with free Wi-Fi, fans, and bedding. The hostel features a kitchen, a dining room, and a terrace, where you may prepare your meals and mix with other guests. The hostel also provides free baggage storage, free maps, and free coffee and tea.

Ostello Corniglia

This hostel is situated in Corniglia, one of the Cinque Terre settlements. It provides mixed dormitories with free Wi-Fi, air conditioning, and bedding. The hostel features a garden, a patio, and a bar, where you can relax and enjoy the surroundings. The hostel also provides cheap entry to the Cinque Terre National Park and free spaghetti evenings.

Cinque Terre provides a choice of lodgings to suit various preferences and budgets. Whether you prefer to stay in a comfortable bed & breakfast, a trendy hotel, a private villa, or a communal hostel, you may find the right location to stay in Cinque Terre. No matter where you choose to stay, you will be surrounded by the beauty and charm of this beautiful location. Enjoy your vacation in Cinque Terre!

What to Pack for Cinque Terre

Cinque Terre is a gorgeous location that provides scenic hiking paths, attractive towns, and wonderful food. But before you pack your bags and fly to this Italian Riviera jewel, there are several things you should know to make your vacation more fun and comfortable.

The weather in Cinque Terre is moderate and sunny most of the year, with modest temperature changes. The Mediterranean Sea moderates the winter season, with an average temperature of 12-14 degrees Celsius. In July, the average temperature exceeds 30 degrees Celsius. The climate is mainly dry, however, rain may occur in spring and fall.

Depending on the season and your activity, you will need various kinds of clothes and gear for your Cinque Terre vacation. Here are some tips about what to pack:

- **For hiking:** Cinque Terre is famed for its network of paths that link the five towns and give stunning views of the coast. Some of the routes are simple and paved, while others are more demanding and steep.

If you wish to trek, you will need comfortable shoes with adequate grip, a hat, sunglasses, sunscreen, water, snacks, and a map or guidebook of the trails. You will also need a Cinque Terre Card, which provides you access to the two most popular trails: from Monterosso to Vernazza and from Vernazza to Corniglia. The membership also offers unlimited rail travel between the settlements and other privileges. You may purchase the card online or at the railway stations.

- **For swimming:** Cinque Terre offers various beaches where you may swim, sunbathe, or hire a kayak or paddle board. The water temperature is warmest in August when it reaches 25 degrees Celsius. If you wish to swim, you will need a swimsuit, a towel, flip-flops, and a waterproof bag for your possessions. Some of the beaches are pebbly or rocky, so you may want to bring water shoes as well.

- **For sightseeing:** Cinque Terre is rich in culture and history, with ancient churches, colorful dwellings, and local art. Each community has its charm and charms. To explore them, you will need comfortable clothing that is suited for the season and the occasion. For example, if you want to attend a church or a museum, you may need to cover your shoulders and knees. You will also need a camera or a phone to capture the splendor of Cinque Terre.

- **For dining:** Cinque Terre is recognized for its seafood, wine, and pesto. You may discover several restaurants, cafés, and taverns that offer these dishes and more. To enjoy them, you will need some cash or a credit card (certain restaurants may not take cards), as well as some basic Italian language to order and speak with the personnel. You may also wish to bring a reusable water bottle or a cup to refill at the public fountains.

- **For emergencies**: Cinque Terre is typically a safe and welcoming location, but accidents and disasters may happen everywhere. To be prepared, you should pack some necessary goods for emergencies, such as a first-aid kit, a flashlight, a whistle, a copy of your passport and travel papers, and your travel insurance data. You should also have the contact details of your embassy or consulate, as well as the local emergency numbers. In Italy, the general emergency number is 112, the medical emergency number is 118, and the fire brigade number is 115.

- **For sustainability:** Cinque Terre is a UNESCO World Heritage Site and a national park, which means it is protected and conserved for its natural and cultural significance. As a responsible tourist, you should respect the environment and the local people by following some basic principles. For example, you should minimize littering, utilize public transit or walk instead of driving, purchase local goods and souvenirs, and preserve water and energy. You should also carry some eco-friendly things, such as a reusable bag, a reusable straw, a bamboo toothbrush, and biodegradable toiletries.

- **For pleasure:** Cinque Terre is not only a destination to admire the beauty and the culture, but also to have fun and enjoy yourself. You may take some things that will make your journey more enjoyable and memorable, such as a book, a diary, a deck of cards, a portable speaker, or a drone (if permitted). You may also bring some presents or mementos for your friends and family back home, such as wine, olive oil, cheese, or pottery.

Cinque Terre is a magnificent place that provides a range of activities and experiences for people of various interests and inclinations. Whether you want to walk, swim, sightsee, or eat, you will find something to enjoy in this wonderful environment. However, to get the most out of your vacation, you need to pack sensibly and suitably for the season, the occasion, and the surroundings.

Cinque Terre is a magnificent place that provides a range of activities and experiences for people of various interests and inclinations. Whether you want to walk, swim, sightsee, or eat, you will find something to enjoy in this wonderful environment. However, to get the most out of your vacation, you need to pack sensibly and suitably for the season, the occasion, and the surroundings.

Visa and entrance requirements

Cinque Terre is a magnificent location in Italy, noted for its colorful towns built on the cliffs overlooking the Ligurian Sea. It is part of the Cinque Terre National Park, a UNESCO World Heritage Site, and provides tourists with a range of activities, including hiking routes, beaches, wineries, and local food. If you are going to visit Cinque Terre in 2023 or 2024, you may be wondering what type of visa and entrance procedures you need to follow. Here is an overview of the essential things you should know before you go.

Do I need a visa to visit Cinque Terre?

The answer depends on your nationality and the purpose and length of your stay. Cinque Terre is situated in Italy, which is part of the Schengen Area, a collection of 27 European nations that have removed border restrictions and allowed free movement of people. If you are a citizen of one of these nations, or the larger EU and EEA, you do not need a visa to visit Italy or any other Schengen country, and there is no restriction on how long you may remain.

If you are not an EU or Schengen citizen, you may still be allowed to visit Cinque Terre without a visa, depending on your place of origin. There are roughly 60 countries outside the EU that have visa-free arrangements with the Schengen Area, including the UK, USA, Canada, Japan, Malaysia, Singapore, New Zealand, and Australia. Citizens of these countries may travel to Italy and other Schengen nations for tourist or business reasons for up to 90 days during any 180 days. Your passport must be valid for at least three months after your anticipated departure date from the Schengen Area, and you may be requested to present evidence of your trip intentions and adequate cash for your stay.

To verify whether your nation is eligible for visa-free travel to Italy, you may use the online tool on the Italian Ministry of Foreign Affairs website. Note that the 90-day restriction applies to the whole Schengen Area, not simply Italy. This implies that if you visit other Schengen countries before or after Cinque Terre, you need to count those days as well. You may use online calculators to keep track of your remaining days in the Schengen Area.

If your country is not on the visa-free list, or if you plan to stay longer than 90 days or work or study in Italy, you will need to apply for a visa in advance. There are numerous sorts of visas based on your position, such as short-stay Schengen visas (up to 90 days), long-stay national visas (more than 90 days), student visas, work visas, family visas, etc. You may discover more information about the various visa categories and criteria on the Italian Ministry of Foreign Affairs website or the website of the Italian embassy or consulate in your country.

What are the Covid-19 admission criteria for Cinque Terre?

Due to the Covid-19 epidemic, Italy has established certain extra entry criteria for tourists from specific countries. These may vary based on epidemiological conditions and government laws, so it is essential to verify the latest developments before you go.

As of July 2023, tourists from EU and Schengen nations may enter Italy without quarantine if they hold one of the following documents:

- A Covid-19 immunization certificate proving that they have finished their vaccine at least 14 days before entering Italy.

- A Covid-19 recovery certificate stating that they have recovered from Covid-19 in the last six months.
- A negative Covid-19 test result (PCR or antigen) performed within 48 hours before entering Italy.

These materials must be in Italian, English, French, or Spanish and may be submitted in digital or paper versions. They must also be registered on the EU Digital Passenger Locator Form (dPLF) before traveling.

Travelers from several non-EU countries that are deemed low-risk may also enter Italy without quarantine if they have one of the aforementioned papers and complete the dPLF. These nations include Australia, Canada, Japan, New Zealand, Singapore, South Korea, and the USA. Travelers from other non-EU countries that are not on the low-risk list may only enter Italy for certain reasons (such as job, health, or study) and must submit a negative Covid-19 test result and undergo a 10-day quarantine upon arrival.

For additional information regarding the Covid-19 entry requirements for Italy, you may visit this official page or contact your airline or travel agency.

Besides having a valid passport and visa (if necessary), there are several additional things you should know before visiting Cinque Terre:

- Cinque Terre is an extremely popular location and might become congested during peak season (from April to October). To protect its natural beauty and cultural history, the Cinque Terre National Park has established several measures to restrict the number of tourists and encourage sustainable tourism. One of these measures is the Cinque Terre Card, a ticket that enables you access to hiking trails, public transit, bathrooms, and other amenities in the area. The Cinque Terre Card is not obligatory, however, it is strongly suggested if you want to experience the finest of Cinque Terre. You may acquire the card online or at railway stations or tourist information centers in Cinque Terre. The fee varies based on the kind and length of the card. For more information on the Cinque Terre Card, you may visit this page.

- Cinque Terre is consists of five villages: Monterosso, Vernazza, Corniglia, Manarola and Riomaggiore. Each hamlet has its beauty and charms, and you may explore them by foot, rail, boat, or bus. The most renowned method to explore Cinque Terre is by trekking along the magnificent routes that link the towns, affording spectacular views of the sea and the environment. However, some of these routes may be closed due to maintenance or weather conditions, so it is essential to verify their status before you go. You can get current information on the trails on this page.

- Cinque Terre is not only about the towns but also about the surrounding region, which provides many other attractions and activities. You may explore surrounding towns such as Levanto, La Spezia, or Portovenere, which have their history and culture. You may also enjoy the water and the beaches, which are great for swimming, snorkeling, or kayaking. You may also try the local cuisine and wine, which are centered on fresh fish, pesto sauce, and lemons. You may get additional information about things to do and see in Cinque Terre on this page.

Visiting Cinque Terre is a fascinating experience that demands some preparation and planning. Depending on your nationality and the purpose and length of your stay, you may require a visa or other documentation to enter Italy and the Schengen Area. You should also verify the Covid-19 entry criteria and limitations that may apply to your journey. In addition, you should be aware of the Cinque Terre Card, the hiking trails, and the numerous attractions and activities that Cinque Terre and its surrounds offer. By following these guidelines, you will be able to experience Cinque Terre to the utmost and have a wonderful vacation.

Currency and Language in Cinque Terre

Cinque Terre is a gorgeous coastal location in the northwest of Italy, comprising five lovely villages: Monterosso al Mare, Vernazza, Corniglia, Manarola, and Riomaggiore. The region is part of the Cinque Terre National Park, a UNESCO globe legacy Site, and draws people from all over the globe who come to appreciate its natural beauty, cultural legacy, and wonderful food.

If you are intending to visit Cinque Terre, you may question what money and language you will need to utilize throughout your vacation. Here are some handy recommendations to help you prepare for your vacation.

Currency

As a member of the European Union, Italy uses the euro (€) as its official currency. You may convert your dollars for euros at exchange kiosks at the airport and railway stations across Cinque Terre. However, you could obtain a better conversion rate if you use your debit or credit card at ATMs, which are generally accessible in villages and adjacent cities. You may also pay with your card at most hotels, restaurants, and stores, but it is best to bring some cash for little purchases, gratuities, and emergencies.

The cost of living in Cinque Terre is very expensive compared to other areas of Italy, owing to its popularity and limited resources. You should expect to spend roughly €15-20 for a dinner at a mid-range restaurant, €3-5 for a coffee or a gelato, €2 for a bottle of water, and €1.50 for a rail ticket between the villages. You may save some money by staying at budget lodgings, making your meals, or purchasing local items at markets and grocery shops.

Tipping is not necessary in Italy, however, it is appreciated if you get excellent service. You may round up the amount or leave 5-10% more in restaurants, cafés, and pubs. You may also tip your hotel personnel, tour guides, taxi drivers, and porters if they are helpful and polite.

Language

The official language of Italy is Italian, although you will find English extensively spoken throughout Cinque Terre villages, notably in hotels and restaurants. However, it is usually polite and acceptable to learn some fundamental words and phrases in Italian before you travel, such as greetings, numbers, directions, and typical queries. You will also impress the locals and increase your trip by demonstrating interest in their culture and history.

Here are some important Italian terms and phrases to get you started:

- Hello: Ciao
- Good morning: Buongiorno
- Good evening: Buonasera
- Good night: Buonanotte
- Goodbye: Arrivederci
- Please: Per favore
- Thank you: Grazie
- You're welcome: Prego
- Excuse me: Scusi
- I'm sorry: Mi dispiace
- Yes: Sì
- No: No
- How are you?: Come stai?
- I'm fine: Sto bene
- What's your name?: Come ti chiami?

- My name is...: Mi chiamo...

- Where are you from?: Di dove sei?

- I'm from...: Sono di...

- Do you speak English?: Parli inglese?

- I don't speak Italian: Non parlo italiano

- I don't understand: Non capisco

- Can you repeat that?: Puoi ripetere?

- How much is it?: Quanto costa?

- Where is...?: Dov'è...?

- Train station: Stazione ferroviaria

- Bus stop: Fermata dell'autobus

- Bathroom: Bagno

- Restaurant: Ristorante

- Hotel: Hotel

- Beach: Spiaggia

- Trail: Sentiero

Another notable characteristic of the language of Cinque Terre is the prevalence of Ligurian dialects, which are spoken by some of the older people and reflect the region's historical and cultural links with Genoa and other areas of Liguria. Ligurian dialects diverge from standard Italian in vocabulary, syntax, pronunciation, and spelling. For example, the name of the place itself is pronounced "Çinque Taere" in Ligurian. You could hear some terms or expressions that seem strange or unintelligible to you, but don't worry - most people will switch to Italian or English if they perceive that you are perplexed.

Learning about the money and language in Cinque Terre can help you organize your vacation better and enjoy your stay more. You will be able to connect with the inhabitants, enjoy their hospitality and customs, and explore the beauty and charm of this unique place.

Suggested Budget

Cinque Terre is a gorgeous area of Italy, where five lovely towns cling to the rough coastline of the Ligurian Sea. It's a popular location for people who wish to explore the beauty, culture, and food of this unique region. But how much does it cost to visit Cinque Terre? And how can you get the most out of your money while enjoying the finest that Cinque Terre has to offer?

The answer depends on your travel style, tastes, and season. Cinque Terre may be an expensive destination to visit, particularly in the high summer months, when accommodation rates spike and visitors throng the small streets and paths. However, there are alternative methods to save money and travel on a budget, without sacrificing quality or pleasure.

In this chapter, we'll provide you with some recommendations and guidance on how to prepare your budget for Cinque Terre, depending on various travel types and conditions. We'll also include some example expenditures for hotel, transport, meals, activities, and more, to help you estimate your spending and plan for your trip.

Travel Styles

We've categorized passengers into three categories: budget, mid-range, and luxury. Of course, these are not set or final labels, but simply basic suggestions to assist you obtain an idea of what type of money you could require for Cinque Terre. You may always mix and combine items from other categories to suit your requirements and tastes.

Budget Travelers

Budget travelers are individuals who strive to save money wherever feasible, without sacrificing too much comfort or convenience. They are happy to stay in basic but hygienic lodging, such as hostels, guesthouses, or campgrounds. They also prefer to utilize public transit or walk instead of renting a vehicle or utilizing cabs. They dine at local eateries or markets or make their meals if they have access to a kitchen. They minimize their expenditure on activities and attractions, preferring free or low-cost choices such as hiking, swimming, or visiting churches.

If you're a budget traveler, you may expect to pay roughly €50–€70 per day in Cinque Terre, depending on the season and availability. This covers lodging, transport, meals, and some activities. Here are some typical expenses for budget vacationers in Cinque Terre:

- **Accommodation:** €20–€40 per night for a dorm bed at a hostel or a camping area. You may also find some private rooms or flats on Airbnb or Booking.com for roughly €50–€60 per night, although these tend to be filled up fast.

- **Transport:** €16 a day for a Cinque Terre Card, which offers you unrestricted access to the trains and buses that link the five villages. You may also trek between the settlements for free, however, certain portions of the paths may demand a charge of €7.50 per day.

- **Food:** €15–€25 per day for breakfast, lunch, and supper at local cafes or markets. You can also purchase food and make your meals if you have access to a kitchen.

- **Activities:** €0–€10 per day for free or low-cost activities such as hiking, swimming, visiting churches or museums. You may even spend on a boat excursion or a wine tasting if you want to pamper yourself.

Mid-Range Travelers

Mid-range travelers are individuals who wish to have a pleasant and easy vacation, without breaking the budget. They are ready to pay more for hotel, transport, and meals than budget tourists, but still strive for value and quality.

They stay in mid-range hotels, B&Bs, or flats that provide private rooms with ensuite bathrooms and facilities such as air conditioning, Wi-Fi, and breakfast. They also utilize a mix of public transit and taxis or vehicle rentals to get about. They dine at modestly priced restaurants or cafés that deliver genuine and good cuisine. They also spend more on activities and attractions that interest them, such as guided tours, kayaking, or culinary lessons.

If you're a mid-range visitor, you may expect to pay roughly €100–€150 per day in Cinque Terre, depending on the season and availability. This covers lodging, transport, meals, and some activities. Here are some typical expenses for mid-range tourists in Cinque Terre:

- **Accommodation:** €60–€100 per night for a double room in a mid-range hotel or B&B with breakfast included. You may also find several flats or villas on Airbnb or Booking.com for roughly €80–€120 per night.

- **Transport:** €16 per day for a Cinque Terre Card (see above), plus €10–€20 per day for taxis or vehicle rentals if you want more flexibility and convenience. You may also hire a bike or a scooter for roughly €15–€25 per day.

- **Food:** €30–€50 a day for breakfast, lunch, and supper at modestly priced restaurants or cafes that provide local specialties like shellfish, pesto, or focaccia. You may also indulge in some gelato, coffee, or wine for an additional delight.

- **Activities:** €10–€30 per day for activities and sights that interest you, such as guided tours, kayaking, culinary lessons, or wine tasting. You may also visit some of the local towns or cities such as Portofino, Pisa, or Florence for a day excursion.

Luxury Travelers

Luxury tourists are individuals who wish to enjoy the finest that Cinque Terre has to offer, without worrying about the expense. They are ready to spend on housing, transport, and meals that provide the greatest levels of comfort, convenience, and quality. They stay at luxury hotels, resorts, or villas that provide huge rooms with spectacular views and facilities such as pools, spas, and restaurants.

They also employ private transports or chauffeured automobiles to go about. They dine at fancy restaurants or bistros that provide gourmet cuisine and wine. They also love special activities and attractions that provide unique and unforgettable experiences, such as private boat cruises, helicopter flights, or spa treatments.

If you're a luxury traveler, you may expect to pay roughly €200–€300 per day in Cinque Terre, depending on the season and availability. This covers lodging, transport, meals, and some activities. Here are some typical expenses for luxury guests in Cinque Terre:

- **Accommodation:** €120–€200 per night for a double room at a premium hotel or resort with breakfast included. You may also discover several villas or penthouses on Airbnb or Booking.com for roughly €150–€250 per night.

- **Transport:** €50–€100 a day for private shuttles or chauffeured vehicles that take you to and from the airport and between the villages. You may also hire a private boat excursion or a helicopter flight for roughly €100–€200 per person.

Cuisine: €50–€80 a day for breakfast, lunch, and supper at premium restaurants or bistros that provide gourmet cuisine and wine. You may also order room service or enjoy a picnic on the beach with local cuisine.

- **Activities:** €30–€50 a day for exclusive activities and attractions that provide unique and memorable experiences, such as private boat trips, helicopter flights, spa treatments, or personal shopping.

Seasonal Variations

The cost of visiting Cinque Terre also fluctuates depending on the season. The peak season is from June through August, when the weather is bright and sunny, but also busy and pricey. The shoulder season is from April to May and from September to October when the weather is moderate and pleasant, but crowded and pricy. The low season is from November through March, when the weather is chilly and wet, but also peaceful and affordable.

Here are some benefits and downsides of visiting Cinque Terre in each season:

- **Peak season (June to August):** The positives are that you may enjoy the ideal weather conditions, with sunny days and mild temperatures. You may also take advantage of the various festivals and events that take place in the summer, such as the Festa del

Mare (Sea Festival) in Monterosso or the Festa della Madonna Bianca (White Madonna Festival) in Portovenere. The drawbacks are that you have to cope with the masses of visitors who swarm to Cinque Terre in the summer, making it hard to obtain lodging, transport, and space on the trails and beaches. You also have to pay higher costs for everything, since demand outweighs supply.

- **Shoulder season (April to May and September to October):** The positives are that you may still enjoy ideal weather conditions, with moderate days and chilly evenings. You can also view the wonderful hues of spring and fall, with flowers budding and leaves changing. The drawbacks are that you still have to confront certain hordes of visitors, particularly during weekends and holidays. You also have to pay greater costs than in the low season, albeit not as expensive as in the peak season.

- **Low season (November to March):** The positives are that you can enjoy Cinque Terre virtually to yourself, with few visitors around. You may also discover fantastic savings on hotel, transit, and food since costs decrease dramatically. The negatives are that you have to contend with severe weather conditions, with chilly days and wet nights. You also have to miss out on certain activities and attractions, since some paths may be blocked due to landslides or maintenance, some ferries may not run owing to stormy seas, and some restaurants may be closed for holidays.

Sample Budgets

To give you a better sense of how much it costs to visit Cinque Terre in various seasons and travel modes, here are some example budgets for a five-day trip:

- **Budget**
- Peak season: €350–€490 for five days, or €70–€98 each day.
- Shoulder season: €300–€400 for five days, or €60–€80 each day.
- Low season: €250–€310 for five days, or €50–€62 each day.
- **Mid-range**

- Peak season: €700–€1050 for five days, or €140–€210 each day.
- Shoulder season: €600–€800 for five days, or €120–€160 each day.
- Low season: €500–€650 for five days, or €100–€130 each day.
- **Luxury**
- Peak season: €1400–€2100 for five days, or €280–€420 each day.
- Shoulder season: €1200–€1600 for five days, or €240–€320 each day.
- Low season: €1000–€1300 for five days, or €200–€260 each day.

These are simply estimates and averages, and your exact expenses may vary based on your unique choices and circumstances. You may always alter your budget according to your choices and demands.

Tips & Advice

Here are some suggestions and advice on how to save money and make the most of your budget in Cinque Terre:

- Book your accommodation in advance, particularly in the peak and shoulder seasons, since costs tend to increase and availability tends to diminish as the date approaches. You may also hunt for offers and discounts on internet sites such as Airbnb or Booking.com, or contact the owners directly to negotiate the price.

- Travel in the low season, if you don't mind the colder and wetter weather, since you may find cheaper accommodation, transport, and food, and experience a more calm and genuine ambiance. You may also escape the crowds and waits that might mar your experience in the peak and shoulder seasons.

- Buy a Cinque Terre Card, if you intend to use the trains and buses regularly, since it may save you money and time. You may also trek between the settlements for free or for a modest cost, depending on the path. However, be aware that certain paths may be blocked due to landslides or maintenance, so check the status before you go.

- Eat like a local, by avoiding tourist eateries that demand excessive rates for substandard cuisine. Instead, seek local cafes or markets that sell fresh and excellent food at affordable costs. You can also purchase food and make your meals if you have access to a kitchen. Some of the local delicacies you should taste include shellfish, pesto, focaccia, farinata, and limoncello.

- Choose your hobbies sensibly, by prioritizing what interests you the most and what matches your budget. You don't have to do all that Cinque Terre has to offer, since certain activities may be costly or overrated. Instead, concentrate on what makes you happy and what gets you the most value for your money. You may also explore free or low-cost activities such as hiking, swimming, or visiting churches.

Money-saving techniques for Cinque Terre

Cinque Terre is a lovely location on the Italian Riviera, noted for its five colorful towns, spectacular hiking paths, and great food. However, it may also be an expensive area to visit, particularly during the high season. Here is some advice on how to save money and enjoy Cinque Terre on a budget.

Travel off-season

The ideal time to visit Cinque Terre is from April to June or from September to October when the weather is beautiful, the crowds are lighter, and the costs are cheaper. Avoid the summer months of July and August, when the region is filled with visitors, the temperatures are high, and the hotel costs are inflated. You may also save money by vacationing in the winter, but be prepared for colder weather, fewer days, and possible closures of restaurants and activities.

Book your accommodation in advance

Cinque Terre is a popular location, so finding an affordable and pleasant place to stay might be tough. The easiest method to score a decent rate is to book your accommodation early in advance, ideally many months before your trip. You may utilize internet sites like Booking.com or Airbnb to compare rates and reviews of various possibilities. Alternatively, you may stay in adjacent cities like Levanto or La Spezia, which are cheaper and less busy than the villages, and readily accessible by rail.

Buy a Cinque Terre Card

If you want to tour Cinque Terre by trekking or utilizing public transit, you might consider getting a Cinque Terre Card. This is a card that enables you unrestricted access to the hiking trails, the regional trains between Levanto and La Spezia, the buses inside the towns, and several museums and attractions. The card costs €16 per day for adults or €29 for two days. You may purchase it online or at any railway station or tourist office in Cinque Terre. The card will save you money and time compared to purchasing individual tickets for each activity.

Eat like a local

One of the greatest ways to save money and appreciate the local culture in Cinque Terre is to eat like a native. This means avoiding tourist restaurants with high pricing and bad quality and choosing real locations that provide fresh and excellent meals. Some of the usual meals you may eat in

Cinque Terre include focaccia (a flat bread with different toppings), pesto (a sauce prepared with basil, garlic, pine nuts, cheese, and olive oil), trofie (a sort of pasta), anchovies (a local delicacy), and sciacchetrà (a sweet wine). You may get these foods from bakeries, grocery shops, street booths, or family-run trattorias. You may also save money by making your meals if you have access to a kitchen at your lodging.

Enjoy free or inexpensive activities

Cinque Terre offers many free or inexpensive activities that you may enjoy without breaking your wallet. For example, you can:

- Take a stroll along the Via dell'Amore (Lovers' Lane), a paved route that links Riomaggiore and Manarola with breathtaking views of the sea.
- Visit the Santuario di Nostra Signora di Montenero (Sanctuary of Our Lady of Montenero), a 14th-century church that overlooks Riomaggiore from a hilltop.

- Explore the Castello Doria (Doria Castle), an ancient fortification that gives panoramic views of Vernazza and its port.
- Relax on the Spiaggia di Fegina (Fegina Beach), the biggest and most popular beach in Monterosso.
- Watch the sunset at Punta Bonfiglio (Bonfiglio Point), a picturesque area above Manarola with a playground and a bar.

These are just some of the ways you may save money and have fun in Cinque Terre.

Best sites to plan your vacation to Cinque Terre

Cinque Terre is a dream destination for many people, but it may also be a struggle to organize and arrange your vacation to this wonderful area. With five communities, dozens of paths, and limited transit choices, you need to do some study and planning before you travel. Here are some suggestions and tools to help you identify the finest sites to plan your vacation to Cinque Terre.

- Decide when to go. Cinque Terre is a year-round attraction, but each season has its benefits and downsides. Summer is the peak season, with bright weather, warm sea, and tonnes of festivals and events, but also with crowds, high costs, and limited availability. Winter is the low season, with milder temperatures, fewer visitors, and reduced costs, but also with certain closures, shorter days, and possibly rain or snow. Spring and fall are the greatest periods to visit Cinque Terre, with moderate weather, fewer people, and more cheap prices.

- Choose where to stay. Cinque Terre provides a range of housing alternatives, from hotels and guesthouses to flats and campsites. You may opt to stay in one of the five villages or one of the neighboring towns or cities. Each choice has its perks and downsides, based on your budget, tastes, and itinerary. Here are some of the finest locations to reserve your hotel in Cinque Terre:

- **Booking.com:** This is one of the most popular and trusted websites to book hotels, guesthouses, flats, and other kinds of accommodation in Cinque Terre. You may filter by location, price, rating, amenities, and availability, and read reviews from other travelers. You might also get offers and discounts on specific homes.

- **Airbnb:** This is an excellent alternative if you wish to stay in a local's home or rent a private apartment or house in Cinque Terre. You may discover distinctive and pleasant accommodations with more space and facilities than a hotel room. You may also interact with the host directly and obtain advice and ideas for your vacation.

- **Hostelworld:** This is the finest website to book hostels, campgrounds, and affordable lodging in Cinque Terre. You may discover affordable and pleasant accommodations with dormitories or individual rooms, common utilities, and a communal environment. You may also read reviews from other backpackers and tourists.

- Plan how to go about it. Cinque Terre is not particularly accessible by automobile, since the roads are tiny, twisting, and frequently blocked. The easiest method to travel around Cinque Terre is via rail or boat, which links the five villages and the neighboring cities. You may also trek between the settlements on the magnificent routes that go along the shore or into the hills. Here are some of the finest locations to schedule your transportation in Cinque Terre:

- **Trenitalia:** This is the official website of the Italian national railway corporation that runs the trains in Cinque Terre. You may purchase tickets online or at the railway stations in each hamlet. You may also check the schedules, rates, and updates on the rail service.

- **Cinque Terre Card:** This is a card that enables you unrestricted access to the trains and trails inside the Cinque Terre National Park for a set fee. You may purchase it online or at any of the railway stations or tourist offices in Cinque Terre. It also includes free Wi-Fi, free use of public bathrooms, free entrance to various museums and attractions, and discounts on some restaurants and stores.

- **Consorzio Marittimo Turistico 5 Terre Golfo dei Poeti:** This is the official website of the ferry business that runs the boats in Cinque Terre. You may purchase tickets online or at the ferry docks in each village. You may also check the schedules, rates, and updates on the boat service.

- Book your activities and experiences. Cinque Terre has a lot to offer besides its breathtaking landscape and quaint communities. You may enjoy many activities and experiences that will make your vacation more memorable and exciting. Here are some of the finest sites to plan your activities and experiences in Cinque Terre:

- **GetYourGuide:** This is a website that provides a broad choice of excursions and activities in Cinque Terre, such as hiking tours, wine-tasting tours, culinary workshops, boat cruises, kayaking tours, photography tours, and more. You may explore by category, price, length, rating, and availability, and read reviews from other travelers.

- **Viator:** This is another website that provides a range of excursions and activities in Cinque Terre, such as sunset cruises, snorkeling tours, fishing tours, cheese-making classes, and more. You may sort by kind, price, rating, and availability, and read reviews from other travelers.

CHAPTER 2

CINQUE TERRE TOP ATTRACTIONS

Cinque Terre is a gorgeous coastal location in the northwest of Italy, comprising five lovely villages: Monterosso al Mare, Vernazza, Corniglia, Manarola, and Riomaggiore. The region is part of the Cinque Terre National Park, a UNESCO globe legacy Site, and draws people from all over the globe who come to appreciate its natural beauty, cultural legacy, and wonderful food.

There are many things to see and do in Cinque Terre, from hiking the gorgeous paths that link the towns, to taking a boat excursion down the coast, to enjoying the fresh seafood and local wines. Here are some of the top sights that you should not miss during your stay.

Monterosso al Mare

Monterosso al Mare is the biggest and most developed of the five settlements and offers the greatest beach amenities. It is separated into two parts: the ancient town and the modern Fegina sector. In the old town, you can visit the Church of San Francesco, a 17th-century monastery that holds paintings by Van Dyck and Cambiaso, and enjoy panoramic views from the Castello Doria, a medieval fortification that overlooks the sea. In Fegina, you may rest on the beautiful Monterosso Beach, or view the huge statue of Neptune that sits on a rocky outcrop.

Vernazza

Vernazza is regarded by many to be the most attractive and picturesque of the five towns, with its colorful buildings gathered around a little port. It has a rich history as a maritime republic and a fishing community, and you can find vestiges of its past in its architecture and culture. You may visit the Church of Santa Margherita d'Antiochia, a 14th-century Gothic church that sits on a peninsula by the sea, or explore the Castello Doria, a 15th-century tower that gives beautiful views of the hamlet and the shore. You may also wander along the waterfront, where you can find cafés, restaurants, and shopping.

Corniglia

Corniglia is the smallest and tallest of the five communities, built on top of a cliff 100 meters above sea level. It is bordered by vineyards and terraced fields and has a more rustic and serene character than the other communities. To access there, you have to climb 377 steps from the railway station or use a shuttle bus. Once there, you may enjoy beautiful views from the Belvedere di Santa Maria, a viewing point that overlooks the sea, or explore the Church of San Pietro, a 14th-century Gothic church that contains a rose window and marble statues. You may also enjoy some of the local specialties, such as honey, wine, and figs.

Manarola

Manarola is one of the oldest and most attractive communities in Cinque Terre, with its buildings clinging to the high cliffs above the sea. It is famed for its Christmas Nativity Scene, which is lit by thousands of lights every year from December through January. It is also noted for its wine production, notably Sciacchetrà, a sweet dessert wine. You may visit the Church of San Lorenzo, a 14th-century Gothic church that has some great paintings and triptychs, or take a stroll to Punta Bonfiglio, a rocky peninsula that gives beautiful views of the hamlet and the ocean. You may also swim in the pristine waters of Fossola Beach, or take a kayak excursion to explore the caves and cliffs.

Riomaggiore

Riomaggiore is the easternmost and est populated of the five settlements and has a bustling and dynamic environment. It is known for its steep alleys and colorful residences that slope down to the sea. You may visit the Church of San Giovanni Battista, one of the oldest churches in Cinque Terre, dating back to 1340, or tour the Castello di Riomaggiore, a 13th-century fortress that holds cultural events and exhibits. You may also stroll down the famed Via dell'Amore, or Lover's Lane, a romantic road that links Riomaggiore with Manarola, affording breathtaking views of the sea and the cliffs.

These are some of the best attractions in Cinque Terre that you should not miss during your vacation. However, there are many more things to explore and enjoy in this great place. You may also take day excursions to surrounding cities such as Portovenere or Levanto, or explore other attractions such as markets, museums, and parks. Whatever you choose to do, you will undoubtedly fall in love with Cinque Terre and its distinct charm.

CHAPTER 3

CINQUE TERRE'S BEST RESTAURANTS AND CAFES

Cinque Terre is heaven for foodies, with a range of foods and tastes to satisfy every pallet. Whether you're searching for a romantic supper, a casual lunch, or a fast nibble, you'll find plenty of alternatives to satiate your tastes. Here are some of the greatest restaurants and cafés in Cinque Terre for 2023-2024, based on ratings, reviews, and popularity.

Cinque Terre provides a broad range of eating alternatives, ranging from traditional cuisine to cosmopolitan cuisines influenced by tastes from throughout the globe.

In this chapter, we will examine some of the top restaurants and cafés in Cinque Terre, including famous spots that are recognized for their imaginative cuisine, good service, and distinctive ambiance.

So, join us as we begin a gastronomic trip around the colorful and delectable island of Cinque Terre.

Traditional Cinque Terre Restaurants

Cinque Terre is heaven for food enthusiasts, with a range of foods and tastes to satisfy every pallet. Whether you're searching for a traditional supper, a seafood feast, or a street food nibble, you'll find lots of alternatives to satiate your needs. Here are some of the greatest traditional restaurants and cafés in Cinque Terre for 2023-2024, based on ratings, reviews, and popularity.

Cinque Terre cuisine is built on the native products of the land and the sea, such as olives, grapes, basil, anchovies, mussels, and tuna. The recipes are simple and healthful, cooked with extra virgin olive oil, fresh veggies, herbs, and cheese. Some of the typical dishes you can try in Cinque Terre are trofie al pesto (fresh pasta with basil sauce), muscoli (mussels cooked in white wine and garlic), acciughe (anchovies served in various ways), focaccia (flatbread with olive oil and salt), farinata (flatbread made from chickpea flour), and sciacchetrà (a sweet wine made from dried grapes).

We will examine some of the greatest traditional restaurants and cafés in Cinque Terre, including famous venues that are recognized for their original food, pleasant service, and attractive ambiance.

Best Restaurants in Riomaggiore

1. **Rio Bistrot:** For the ultimate seafood supper with a waterfront view. Make sure you reserve a table here, otherwise, you won't get a space (this is true for most restaurants in Cinque Terre unless you are willing to wait for a long time). The menu varies every few days to make the most of the local products available. You ought to try the handmade pasta with mussels (called muscoli locally).

2. **A Pie' de Ma':** With a very romantic setting (Lovers' Lane) facing the sea, this restaurant provides a tiny range of local cuisine but the quality of the ingredients is spot on. The site is wonderful, particularly around sunset. You may sample the octopus salad, the tuna tartare, or the fish soup.

3. **La Grotta:** A quaint and rustic restaurant that offers traditional Ligurian food with a twist. The servings are large and the pricing is fair. You may sample the

stuffed mussels, the anchovies with lemon sauce, or the rabbit with olives.

Best Restaurants in Manarola

1. **Trattoria Dal Billy:** My favorite restaurant in Cinque Terre, particularly for the magnificent view. It takes a bit of a climb, but it's well worth it. You will need to book if you go in the evening. You can either go at 7:30 pm or 9:00 pm, they only have 2 table seatings at this time (I know...odd), but the fish is excellent and fresh, and the pasta is amazing. You may try the taglierini with shrimp and pine nuts, the grilled swordfish, or the mixed-fried fish.

2. **Nessun Dorma:** A popular place for a drink or a snack with a wonderful view of Manarola. You may have a drink of local wine or a cocktail with some appetizers like bruschetta, cheese plate, or pesto pasta. The location is frequently busy and loud, but the atmosphere is energetic and entertaining.

3. **Il Porticciolo:** A family-run restaurant that provides traditional cuisine with fresh vegetables

from their garden. The service is kind and attentive, and the ambiance is pleasant and sophisticated. You may sample the ravioli with walnut sauce, the sea bass with potatoes, or the tiramisu.

Best Restaurants in Corniglia

1. **Alberto Gelateria:** A must-stop for gelato fans in Cinque Terre. This gelateria creates its ice cream using natural ingredients and no artificial flavors. The tastes are rich and creamy and alter according to the season. You may sample the basil gelato, the fig gelato, or the honey gelato.

2. **Osteria La Torpedine:** A quaint eatery that offers fresh fish and handmade pasta with innovative sauces. The service is courteous and professional, and the servings are ample. You may sample the spaghetti with clams and bottarga (dried fish roe), the squid ink ravioli with shrimp sauce, or the grilled octopus with potatoes.

3. **Terra Rossa Wine Bar:** A quiet wine bar that provides a range of local wines and beers, along with

some nibbles and small dinners. The staff is informed and friendly, and the ambiance is calm and pleasant. You may sample the cheese and salami plate, the veggie quiche, or the focaccia with pesto.

Best Restaurants in Vernazza

1. **Il Pirata delle Cinque Terre:** A vibrant and colorful restaurant that provides wonderful seafood and pasta meals, as well as pastries and sweets. The proprietors are two brothers from Sicily who are incredibly nice and engaging. The location is typically loud and noisy, but the meal is worth the wait. You may try the linguine with fish, the fried calamari, or the cannoli.

2. **Ristorante Belforte:** A charming restaurant that gives a wonderful view of Vernazza and the sea. The menu comprises marine delicacies and classic meals with a contemporary twist. The service is pleasant and fast, and the costs are reasonable. You may sample the risotto with scampi, the swordfish steak, or the lemon cake.

3. **Pippo a Vernazza:** A informal and pleasant establishment that provides street cuisine and local recipes with a twist. The menu varies every day according to the availability of fresh products. The meals are modest yet good, and the costs are affordable. You may sample the anchovy sandwich, the tuna salad, or the oysters.

Best Restaurants in Monterosso al Mare

1. **La Cantina del Pescatore:** A modest and rustic restaurant that offers traditional seafood dishes with an emphasis on quality and freshness. The service is responsive and friendly, and the environment is warm and pleasant. You may sample the tuna carpaccio, the seafood risotto, or the mixed grilled fish.

2. **Enoteca does Eliseo:** A wine bar that serves a range of local wines and beers, along with some appetizers and small meals. The staff is informed and helpful, and the ambiance is casual and homey. You may sample the cheese and ham plate, the veggie pie, or the focaccia with cheese.

3. **Il Frantoio:** A pizzeria that provides wonderful pizzas and focaccias with varied toppings. The bread is thin and crunchy, and the fillings are fresh and tasty. The service is quick and efficient, and the costs are affordable. You may sample the tomato and anchovy pizza, the cheese focaccia, or the Nutella pizza.

These are only some of the top traditional restaurants and cafés in Cinque Terre for 2023-2024.

Cinque Terre, the five lovely towns on the Ligurian coast, is not only a UNESCO World Heritage Site and a magnificent location for hiking, swimming, and sightseeing but also a dream for culinary lovers. The local cuisine is built on fresh fish, fragrant herbs, olive oil, and of course, pesto, the renowned basil sauce that originated in this area. Whether you are searching for a romantic supper with a view, a quaint trattoria with traditional dishes, or a contemporary location with unique fusion food, you will find plenty of alternatives to suit your palette in Cinque Terre. Here are some of the top restaurants in each community, according to the people and the reviewers.

Corniglia

1. **A Cantina de Mananan:** This quaint and rustic restaurant is located in one of the short lanes of Corniglia, the smallest and highest hamlet of Cinque Terre. The menu contains characteristic Ligurian delicacies such as trofie al pesto (twisted pasta with pesto), stuffed mussels, and anchovies in different ways. The servings are big and the service is courteous.

2. **Terra Rossa:** This wine bar is set in a picturesque plaza with a fountain and provides a superb range of local wines and cheeses. You may also enjoy salads, sandwiches, and desserts produced using organic ingredients. The environment is easygoing and pleasant.

Vernazza

1. **Gianni Franzi:** This restaurant is part of a hotel that covers many buildings on Vernazza's main plaza, near the harbor. You may eat on the balcony overlooking the sea or in one of the internal rooms filled with murals and antiques. The cuisine features seafood delicacies such as pasta with lobster, grilled octopus, and swordfish carpaccio.

2. **Il Pirata delle Cinque Terre:** This family-run restaurant is situated on the higher portion of Vernazza, near the railway station. It provides a range of foods from breakfast to supper, but it's most renowned for its pastries and cakes produced by the two Sicilian brothers who run it. You may also

sample their seafood delicacies such as salmon linguine, tuna tartare, and oysters.

Monterosso al Mare

1. **Miky:** This exquisite restaurant is situated in Fegina, the newer area of Monterosso al Mare, near the beach. It delivers excellent and imaginative cuisine based on local ingredients and seafood. Some of their hallmark dishes include risotto with prawns and strawberries, squid ink tagliatelle with cuttlefish ragout, and fried anchovies with lemon cream.

2. **La Cantina del Pescatore:** This relaxed and welcoming restaurant is situated in the ancient town of Monterosso al Mare, near the church of San Giovanni Battista. It specializes in fish and seafood delicacies such as tuna salad, focaccia sandwiches, grilled sardines, and mixed-fried fish. You may also drink the local wine Sassarini here.

Cinque Terre is a place that will please your senses with its natural beauty, cultural legacy, and gourmet pleasures. Whether you like a basic and traditional dinner or a refined and imaginative one, you will find a restaurant that meets your taste and budget in each of the five villages. Don't miss the chance to experience the local delicacies such as pesto, anchovies, mussels, and wine, and to appreciate the breathtaking views of the sea and the hills. Cinque Terre is a destination where cuisine and landscape are equally remarkable.

Cafes and bakeries

Cinque Terre is not only a feast for the eyes, but also for the taste sensations. The area is noted for its fresh and tasty cuisine, notably its seafood, pesto, and focaccia. But whether you're searching for something sweet or savory to start your day, or to enjoy as a snack or dessert, you'll be thrilled by the variety and quality of cafés and bakeries that dot the five towns.

Whether you're wanting a croissant, a cake, a cookie, or a pie, you'll find something to satiate your sweet taste in Cinque Terre. And if you're more into savory delicacies, you'll appreciate the local favorites such as farinata, torta di verdure, or panissa. Of course, you can't miss the opportunity to drink the famed limoncello, a liqueur derived from the lemons that grow abundantly in the region.

In this chapter, we'll introduce you to some of the greatest cafés and bakeries in Cinque Terre, where you can indulge in exquisite pastries, bread, cakes, and more. We'll also provide you with some ideas and suggestions on how to order, pay, and tip at these businesses.

Best cafés and bakeries in Cinque Terre

Here are some of the top cafés and bakeries in Cinque Terre, categorized by village. Note that some of these may have restricted opening hours or seasonal closures, so verify before you go.

Monterosso

Monterosso is the biggest and most developed of the five villages, and it offers lots of cafés and bakeries to pick from. Here are some of our favorites:

1. **Pasticceria Laura:** This tiny and attractive pastry store is situated near the railway station, and it provides a broad assortment of cakes, pies, pastries, and more. You may also request custom-made cakes for special events. Try their famous torta Monterossina, a sponge cake with cream and chocolate.

2. **Il Fornaio di Monterosso:** This bakery is famed for its focaccia, a flat bread topped with different toppings like cheese, olives, or tomatoes. You may purchase it by the slice or by weight, and enjoy it as a

snack or a meal. They also offer various breads, pizzas, and pastries.

3. **Gelateria Golosone:** This gelateria is situated on the main street of the old town, and it provides some of the greatest gelatos in Cinque Terre. They employ natural ingredients and local goods to produce their creamy and tasty gelato. You may select from standard flavors such as chocolate or vanilla, or try some of their specialties like lemon or basil.

Vernazza

Vernazza is one of the most scenic and popular settlements in Cinque Terre, and it offers several cafés and bakeries that match its attractiveness. Here are some of our favorites:

1. **Pasticceria Vernazza:** This pastry store is situated near the port, and it has a nice patio where you can enjoy your delicacies with a view of the sea. They provide a range of pastries, cakes, cookies, and more. Try their torta di riso, a rice cake with custard and pine nuts.

2. **Batti Batti:** This café is situated in the main plaza of the hamlet, and it offers a warm and calm environment. They provide coffee, tea, juice, sandwiches, salads and more. Try their focaccia al Formaggio di Recco, a thin crust stuffed with cheese.

3. **Gelateria Il Porticciolo:** This gelateria is situated on the waterfront, and it features a tiny yet appealing assortment of gelato varieties. They utilize fresh ingredients and no artificial colors or flavors to manufacture their gelato. You may select from tastes such as pistachio, hazelnut, or strawberry.

Corniglia

Corniglia is the smallest and tallest of the five settlements, and it offers a few cafés and bakeries that are worth the trip. Here are some of our favorites:

1. **Pasticceria Pan e Vin:** This pastry store is situated near the bus stop that brings you to Corniglia from the railway station, and it has a charming and friendly decor. They provide a range of pastries, cakes, cookies, and more. Try their millefoglie alla

crema chantilly e fragole, a puff pastry with whipped cream and strawberries.

2. **Bar Nunzio:** This café is situated on the main street of the hamlet, and it has a big and sunny patio where you can enjoy your beverages and food. They provide coffee, tea, juice, sandwiches, salads and more. Try their farinata, a thin pancake made from chickpea flour and oil.

3. **Alberto Gelateria:** This gelateria is nestled on a side street in the hamlet, and it features a modest but colorful display of gelato varieties. They utilize natural ingredients and local goods to manufacture their gelato. You may select from tastes such as lemon, peach, or almond.

Manarola

Manarola is one of the most gorgeous and charming settlements in Cinque Terre, and it boasts various cafés and bakeries that are excellent for a sweet stop. Here are some of our favorites:

1. **Pasticceria Cinque Terre: This** pastry store is situated near the church, and it boasts a contemporary and stylish atmosphere. They provide a range of pastries, cakes, cookies, and more. Try their torta di ricotta e cioccolato, a ricotta cheese and chocolate cake.

2. **Nessun Dorma:** This café is perched on a cliff overlooking the sea, and it boasts a wonderful view of the hamlet and the shore. They provide coffee, tea, juice, sandwiches, salads and more. Try their panissa fritta, a fried delicacy made from chickpea flour.

3. **Gelateria 5 Terre:** This gelateria is situated on the main street of the hamlet, and it features a big and tempting assortment of gelato varieties. They utilize natural ingredients and local goods to manufacture their gelato. You may select from tastes such as mango, coconut, or pistachio.

Riomaggiore

Riomaggiore is the southernmost and most vibrant of the five towns, and it offers lots of cafés and pastries to keep you energetic. Here are some of our favorites:

1. **Pasticceria La Dolce Vita:** This pastry store is situated near the railway station, and it boasts a colorful and cheery ambiance. They provide a range of pastries, cakes, cookies, and more. Try their torta di mele e cannella, an apple, and cinnamon cake.

2. **Bar Centrale:** This café is situated on the main street of the hamlet, and it offers a relaxed and pleasant environment. They provide coffee, tea, juice, sandwiches, salads and more. Try their torta di verdure, a vegetable pie.

3. **Gelateria Il Pinguino:** This gelateria is situated on the waterfront, and it offers a charming and colorful display of gelato varieties. They utilize natural ingredients and local goods to manufacture their gelato. You may select from tastes such as raspberry, banana, or caramel.

Tips & Advice

Here are some suggestions and recommendations on how to enjoy the cafés and bakeries in Cinque Terre:

- Order in Italian, if you can, or at least learn some fundamental words and phrases such as buongiorno (good morning), grazie (thank you), or per favore (please). The locals will appreciate your effort and may even offer you a grin or a discount.

- Pay in cash, if feasible, or use a credit card that doesn't incur international transaction fees. Some cafés and bakeries may not take cards or may charge additional fees for using them.

- Tip generously, if you're delighted with the service and the quality of the meal. Tipping is not mandated in Italy, however, it's traditional to leave roughly 10% of the bill or round up to the closest euro.

CHAPTER 4

Cinque Terre Nightlife & Entertainment

Cinque Terre may not be the ideal spot to go if you are seeking crazy and bustling nightlife, but that doesn't mean you can't have fun once the sun sets. Cinque Terre boasts a pleasant and calm nightlife that matches its natural and cultural appeal. You may have a drink with a view, listen to some live music, or attend a local festival or event. Here are some ideas and recommendations to help you make the most of your Cinque Terre nightlife and entertainment.

Bars and pubs

Cinque Terre features a few bars and pubs where you may drink a glass of wine, beer, or cocktail, and mix with other visitors and residents. Most of them shut about midnight, save for a couple in Monterosso and Riomaggiore that remain open until 1 a.m. or later. Some of the top bars and pubs in Cinque Terre are:

A Pié de Mà in Riomaggiore

This is a tiny and charming pub on a cliff overlooking the sea. You may have a drink on the patio while enjoying the sunset or the stars. It also provides wonderful cuisine and snacks.

- Nessun Dorma in Manarola: This is a popular and fashionable pub with a wonderful view of the town and the shore. You may get cool beverages, local wines, and excellent snacks. It also features live music on various evenings.

Blue Marlin Bar in Vernazza

This is a busy and welcoming bar with a terrace on the main street. You may listen to live music, karaoke, or DJ performances, and dance with the audience. It also features a nice assortment of beverages and snacks.

Live music & concerts.

Cinque Terre has a strong musical culture, including folk and classical music. You may discover live music performances in select taverns, restaurants, churches, or squares throughout the year. Some of the greatest spots to experience live music and concerts in Cinque Terre are:

Oratorio di Santa Caterina in Vernazza

This is a lovely 14th-century church that holds classical music performances every week from June to September. You may listen to skilled performers performing piano, violin, cello, guitar, flute, and more.

La Scuna in Corniglia

This is a charming and rustic restaurant that provides live music every night from July to September. You may hear local musicians performing rock, blues, jazz, reggae, and more.

pub Centrale in Monterosso

This is a relaxed and contemporary pub that presents live music every weekend from May to October. You may enjoy rock, pop, indie, and acoustic music from local and worldwide musicians.

- Festivals and events. Cinque Terre boasts a rich and colorful cultural environment, with various festivals and events honoring its history, customs, religion, cuisine, wine, and art. You may attend these festivals and activities to experience the real spirit and delight of Cinque Terre. Some of the greatest festivals and events in Cinque Terre are:

Festa del Limone (Lemon event) at Monterosso

This is an annual event that takes place in May to honor the lemon, one of the most significant products of Cinque Terre. You may observe lemon-themed décor, displays, competitions, activities, and tastings.

Festa di San Giovanni Battista (Feast of Saint John the Baptist) in Riomaggiore:

This is an annual celebration that takes place on June 24th to honor the patron saint of Riomaggiore. You may observe religious processions, pyrotechnics, music, and dancing.

Festa della Madonna Bianca (Feast of the White Madonna) in Portovenere

This is an annual celebration that takes place on August 17th to celebrate a miracle that happened in 1399 when an image of the Virgin Mary appeared on a rock near the sea. You can see hundreds of lights lighting the community, the castle, and the church of San Pietro.

Cinque Terre has a lot to offer for people who are searching for nightlife and entertainment that is distinct from the ordinary. You may have a drink with a view, listen to some live music, or attend a local festival or event. You may also explore the culture and customs of Cinque Terre pleasantly and genuinely.

CHAPTER 5

SHOPPING IN CINQUE TERRE

Cinque Terre is not only a haven for nature lovers and foodies, but also for shoppers who are searching for some unique and local things to take home. Whether you're searching for souvenirs, handicrafts, art, or cuisine, you'll find lots of alternatives to fit your taste and budget. Here are some of the top venues and marketplaces to shop in Cinque Terre for 2023-2024, based on ratings, reviews, and popularity.

Cinque Terre shopping is focused on the local culture and traditions of the region, such as olive oil, wine, pesto, anchovies, pottery, paintings, and jewelry. You may find these things at numerous stores and booths in the villages, as well as in the weekly markets that take place in different places. You may also tour other surrounding towns that provide a greater variety and quality of items, such as La Spezia, Chiavari, and Sarzana.

In this chapter, we will examine some of the greatest locations and marketplaces to shop in Cinque Terre, including famous establishments that are recognized for their original items, pleasant service, and attractive ambiance.

Best Places to Shop in Riomaggiore

- **Gocce di Byron:** A little business that offers handcrafted soaps, fragrances, candles, and cosmetics manufactured with natural materials and inspired by the aromas of Cinque Terre. The goods are elegantly wrapped and make fantastic presents for yourself or your loved ones.

- **Explora:** A business that specialized in outdoor gear and clothes for hiking, bicycling, kayaking, and other activities in Cinque Terre. The personnel is informed and friendly, and the costs are affordable. You may also rent equipment or schedule trips here.

- **Fioravanti Fotografie:** A business that shows the amazing images of Cinque Terre created by local artist Marco Fioravanti. You may purchase prints, posters, postcards, calendars, or books showcasing his art. The store also offers various items including magnets, mugs, and t-shirts.

Best Places to Shop in Manarola

- **Fabbrica d'Arte Monterosso:** A boutique that offers lovely ceramics and paintings produced by local artisans. The items are bright and distinctive, and represent the culture and nature of Cinque Terre. You may get plates, bowls, mugs, vases, tiles, magnets, decorations, and more.

- **MG cinque terre:** A business that offers handcrafted jewelry and accessories created with natural materials including stones, shells, wood, and leather. The items are attractive and distinctive and available in many designs and hues. You may discover earrings, necklaces, bracelets, rings, belts, purses, and more.

- **Cantina du Sciacchetra:** A business that offers local wines and liquors created with grapes from Cinque Terre. The items are great quality and tasty, and available in many varieties and sizes. You may discover white wine (Cinque Terre DOC), red wine (Rossese di Dolceacqua), sweet wine (Sciacchetrà), lemon liqueur (Limoncino), and more. You may also try various samples before purchasing.

Best Places to Shop in Corniglia

- **Alberto Gelateria:** A store that offers handcrafted gelato prepared with natural ingredients and no artificial flavors. The tastes are rich and creamy and alter according to the season. You may get traditional varieties like chocolate or vanilla, as well as local ones like basil or fig. You may also purchase various jars of jam or honey prepared with fruits from Cinque Terre.

- **Terra Rossa Wine Bar:** A business that offers local wines and beers from Cinque Terre and other areas of Italy. The staff is informed and helpful, and the ambiance is casual and homey. You may discover white wine (Cinque Terre DOC), red wine (Rossese di

Dolceacqua), sweet wine (Sciacchetrà), beer (Birra del Borgo), and more. You may also have some snacks or small meals here.

Best Places to Shop in Vernazza

- **Il Pirata delle Cinque Terre:** A store that offers pastries and sweets produced by the proprietors, two brothers from Sicily. The items are excellent and fresh and available in numerous flavors and forms. You may discover cannoli, croissants, cakes, pies, cookies, and more. You may also drink some coffee or tea here.

- **Ristorante Belforte:** A business that offers local items and souvenirs from Cinque Terre. The items are excellent quality and real, and available in many variations and pricing. You may discover olive oil, wine, pesto, anchovies, cheese, honey, jam, spices, and more. You may also purchase various t-shirts, caps, magnets, or postcards here.

- **Pippo a Vernazza:** A store that offers street food and local cuisine from Cinque Terre. The items are excellent and affordable and available in varied amounts and combinations. You may discover an anchovy sandwich, tuna salad, oysters, mussels, fried fish, and more. You may also drink some wine or beer here.

Best Places to Shop in Monterosso al Mare

- **La Cantina del Pescatore:** A business that offers fresh seafood and fish from Cinque Terre. The items are excellent quality and tasty, and available in many sorts and sizes. You can find tuna, swordfish, sea bass, octopus, squid, shrimp, clams, mussels, and more. You may also order certain prepared items here.

- **Enoteca da Eliseo:** A business that offers local wines and beers from Cinque Terre and other areas of Italy. The staff is informed and helpful, and the ambiance is casual and homey. You may discover white wine (Cinque Terre DOC), red wine (Rossese di Dolceacqua), sweet wine (Sciacchetrà), beer (Birra del Borgo), and more. You may also eat some cheese or ham plate here.

- **Il Frantoio:** A store that offers handmade pizzas and focaccias with varied toppings from Cinque Terre. The items are excellent and crispy and available in numerous flavors and sizes. You may discover tomato and anchovy pizza, cheese focaccia, veggie focaccia, Nutella pizza, and more. You may also get various salads or beverages here.

These are only some of the greatest venues and marketplaces to shop in Cinque Terre for 2023-2024.

CHAPTER 6

OUTDOOR ACTIVITIES IN CINQUE TERRE

Cinque Terre, the five picturesque towns on the Ligurian coast, is not only a site to admire the colorful buildings, the terraced vineyards, and the breathtaking sea vistas but also a destination for outdoor lovers who wish to discover the natural beauty and the cultural history of this region. Whether you are searching for a peaceful or adventurous activity, you will find lots of opportunities to enjoy the outdoors in Cinque Terre. Here are some of the top outdoor activities in each community, according to the inhabitants and the reviewers.

Riomaggiore

- **Hiking:** Riomaggiore is the beginning point of one of the most renowned and picturesque routes in Cinque Terre, the Via dell'Amore (Lovers' walk), which links it to Manarola. This accessible and paved trail provides lovely views of the sea and the cliffs, as well as seats and artwork along the way. You may also climb from Riomaggiore to Portovenere, a longer and more demanding path that goes through the communities of Campiglia and Biassa and gives panoramic views of the Gulf of Poets.

- **Scuba Diving:** Riomaggiore is one of the greatest sites for scuba diving in Cinque Terre, owing to its clean and rich waters, where you may meet diverse marine animals such as octopus, moray eels, groupers, and lobsters. You may join a diving center that offers guided dives for various levels, or rent your equipment and explore the underwater world on your own. Some of the most popular diving sites include Il Gabbiano, La Grotta dei Gamberi, and Il Relitto del Tino.

Manarola

- **Sea Kayaking:** Manarola is a terrific site to experience sea kayaking, a fun and eco-friendly way to explore the coast and its hidden beauties. You may hire a kayak and paddle along the rocky beach, appreciating the colorful cottages of Manarola from a fresh viewpoint, or join a guided trip that will take you to nearby towns such as Corniglia and Vernazza, where you can stop for a swim or a lunch. You may also select a sunset or a night trip, where you can experience the magnificent ambiance of Cinque Terre beneath the stars.

Freediving: Manarola is also a fantastic site for freediving, a sport that includes diving without any breathing gear, depending solely on your lungs and your talents. Freediving is a method to feel a deeper connection with yourself and the marine environment, as well as to test your limitations and enhance your well-being. You may join a freediving school that provides lessons and trips for all levels, or practice on your own if you have adequate expertise and equipment. Some of the greatest freediving spots include La Grotta Azzurra, Il Faraglione, and La Parete dei Coralli.

Corniglia

- **Biking:** Corniglia is the only hamlet in Cinque Terre that is not immediately on the sea, but on top of a hill surrounded by vineyards and olive trees. This makes it a great area for riding, as you can enjoy the rural environment and the fresh air while cycling on calm roads or dirt trails. You may hire a bike or an e-bike and explore the countryside on your own, or join a guided tour that will show you the greatest sites and teach you more about the local culture and history. You may also cycle from Corniglia to neighboring towns like Vernazza or Monterosso al Mare if you are searching for additional challenges and diversity.

- **Wine Tasting:** Corniglia is also noted for its wine production, notably the white wine created from the local grape type called Vermentino. Wine tasting is a terrific opportunity to savor the local tastes and customs, as well as to learn more about the winemaking process and history. You may visit one of the numerous vineyards or wine bars in Corniglia, where you can experience various wines combined with cheese, salami, focaccia, and other characteristic goods. You may also join a wine trip that will take you to several vineyards and cellars in Cinque Terre, where you can meet the winemakers and enjoy the views.

Vernazza

- **Boat Tours:** Vernazza is one of the most gorgeous settlements in Cinque Terre, with its colorful buildings gathered around a little port and a castle overlooking the sea. A boat excursion is a fantastic opportunity to appreciate Vernazza from a fresh aspect, as well as to discover other towns and secret bays along the coast. You may hire a boat or a kayak and travel on your own, or join a boat trip that will take you to the greatest sites and teach you more about the history and culture of Cinque Terre. You may also select a fishing trip, where you can learn how to catch and prepare the local fish, or a sunset tour, where you can enjoy the romantic setting and a bottle of wine.

Snorkeling: Vernazza is also a fantastic spot for snorkeling since its waters are clean and rich with life. You may hire snorkeling equipment and explore the underwater world on your own, or join a snorkeling trip that will take you to the finest sites and show you the aquatic richness of Cinque Terre. You may observe colorful fish, corals, starfish, sea urchins, and more. Snorkeling is a fun and simple hobby that everyone can perform, as long as they know how to swim and breathe through a tube.

Monterosso al Mare

- **Beach Activities:** Monterosso al Mare is the biggest and most developed hamlet in Cinque Terre, and it features the longest and sandiest beach in the region. Here you may enjoy a range of beach sports, such as swimming, sunbathing, surfing, windsurfing, stand-up paddle boarding, and more. You may rent equipment and take lessons from one of the numerous beach clubs or surf schools, or simply relax and have fun on your own. You may also wander down the promenade that links the old town with the modern town, where you can find stores, cafés, restaurants, and gelaterias.

- **Paragliding:** Monterosso al Mare is also an excellent spot for paragliding, an exhilarating sport that includes soaring in the air with a parachute tied to your body. Paragliding is a chance to enjoy Cinque Terre from a bird's eye perspective, as well as to feel the adrenaline rush and the freedom of soaring. You may join a paragliding school that provides tandem flights with an instructor, or solo flights if you have appropriate experience and license. You will take off from a hill above Monterosso al Mare and soar above the coast, enjoying the beautiful views of the sea and the towns.

Parks and Gardens

Cinque Terre is a location of natural beauty, where the sea meets the mountains, and where the land is farmed with vineyards, olive groves, and citrus orchards. But if you're searching for some green areas to rest, unwind and enjoy the fresh air, you'll also discover some great parks and gardens in and around the five villages.

Whether you're searching for a picnic site, a playground, a botanical garden, or a historical park, you'll find something to fit your mood and taste at Cinque Terre. In this chapter, we'll introduce you to some of the greatest parks and gardens in Cinque Terre, where you may appreciate the flora and fauna, learn about the history and culture, or just have some fun.

Best parks and gardens in Cinque Terre

Here are some of the nicest parks and gardens in Cinque Terre, arranged by Hamlet. Note that some of these may have restricted opening hours or seasonal closures.

Monterosso

Monterosso is the biggest and most developed of the five villages, and it includes several parks and gardens that give a contrast to its urban air. Here are some of our favorites:

- **Giardini di Villa Montale:** This garden is situated in the villa where the Nobel Prize-winning poet Eugenio Montale spent his summers. It's a tranquil and lovely area, where you can view some of his possessions, such as his typewriter and his books. You may also appreciate the views of the sea and the hills from the terrace.

- **Parco Nazionale delle Cinque Terre:** This park contains the whole area of Cinque Terre, and it's a UNESCO World Heritage Site. It's a paradise for environment enthusiasts, who may explore its different landscapes, from rocky cliffs to sandy beaches, from terraced farms to forested hills. You may also trek along its famed routes, such as the Sentiero Azzurro (Blue Trail) or the Sentiero Rosso (Red Trail).

- **Parco Giochi Fegina:** This playground is situated near the beach of Fegina, and it's a perfect area for youngsters to have some fun. It features swings, slides, seesaws, and more. It also features a snack bar and a restroom.

Vernazza

Vernazza is one of the most attractive and popular settlements in Cinque Terre, and it includes various parks and gardens that add to its beauty. Here are some of our favorites:

- **Giardino Botanico Hanbury:** This botanical garden is situated on a hill above Vernazza, and it's part of the University of Genoa. It's a lovely and instructive area, where you can observe over 300 varieties of plants from throughout the globe. You may also read about their applications and advantages for people and animals.

- **Piazza Marconi:** This piazza is situated in front of the port, and it's the center of Vernazza. It's a vibrant and colorful spot, where you can see residents and visitors socializing, fishing boats docking, and merchants selling their wares. You may also relax on one of the seats or stairs and enjoy the view of the sea and the hamlet.

Corniglia

Corniglia is the smallest and tallest of the five settlements, and it contains various parks and gardens that give a panoramic view of the environs. Here are some of our favorites:

- **Belvedere Santa Maria: This** viewpoint is situated at the end of the main street of Corniglia, and it gives a spectacular view of the sea and the coast. It's a fantastic site to observe the sunset or snap some shots.

- **Orto Botanico di Corniglia:** This botanical garden is situated near the church of San Pietro, and it's operated by volunteers. It's a little but attractive location, where you can view numerous flora that thrives in Cinque Terre, such as lavender, rosemary, or sage. You may also purchase certain items manufactured from these plants, such as soap or honey.

Manarola

Manarola is one of the most attractive and charming settlements in Cinque Terre, and it boasts several parks and gardens that match its splendor. Here are some of our favorites:

- **Giardino di Manarola:** This garden is situated on a hill above Manarola, and it's part of an eco-friendly initiative that tries to conserve and promote the local culture and ecology. It's a lush and tranquil spot, where you can view numerous flora and flowers that bloom in Cinque Terre, such as lemon, olive, or grape. You may also learn about the history and customs of Hamlet, such as the nativity scene that is shown every year.

- **Piazza Capellini:** This plaza is situated in the middle of Manarola, and it's a bustling and colorful spot, where you can watch the inhabitants and visitors chatting, shopping, or eating. You may also enjoy the architecture and the art of the settlement, such as the cathedral of San Lorenzo or the mural of the fallen warriors.

Riomaggiore

Riomaggiore is the southernmost and most vibrant of the five towns, and it boasts lots of parks and gardens to keep you busy. Here are some of our favorites:

- **Giardino di Riomaggiore:** This garden is situated near the castle of Riomaggiore, and it's part of a cultural group that arranges events and activities for the neighborhood. It's a pleasant and imaginative spot, where you can observe numerous plants and sculptures that embellish the space. You may also attend various courses or performances that take place in the garden.

- **Piazza Vignaioli:** This square is situated near the railway station, and it's a contemporary and lovely site, where you can view a fountain that reflects the wine industry of Cinque Terre. You may also rest on one of the seats or chairs and enjoy the environment.

Tips & Advice

Here are some hints and recommendations on how to enjoy the parks and gardens in Cinque Terre:

- Check the opening hours and pricing of the parks and gardens before you go, since they may change based on the season or the day. Some of them may need a reservation or a ticket to attend.

- Respect the norms and regulations of the parks and gardens, such as not littering, not plucking flowers or fruits, and not creating noise or upsetting animals. Be careful of your influence on the environment and the culture.

- Bring some water, food, sunscreen, a cap, and suitable shoes when you visit the parks and gardens, since you may spend some time walking, hiking, or exploring. You may also wish to bring a camera or binoculars to capture the magnificence of the surroundings.

Archipelago tour in Cinque Terre

One of the greatest ways to explore the splendor of Cinque Terre is to join an archipelago cruise that will take you to the islands of Palmaria, Tino, and Tinetto, as well as the gorgeous port of Portovenere. These islands are part of the UNESCO World Heritage Site that encompasses the Cinque Terre and provide breathtaking vistas, rich history, and varied species. Here is a draft of the chapter that I have prepared based on the online search results.

- What to anticipate from an archipelago cruise. An archipelago cruise is a boat trip that begins from Portovenere or La Spezia and rounds around the three islands of Palmaria, Tino, and Tinetto, before returning to Portovenere. The trip lasts around an hour and a half and enables you to view the beauty, learn about the history and culture of the islands, and identify some of the uncommon birds and flora that inhabit there. You may also opt to combine the trip with a stop in Portovenere, where you can tour its historic castle, a Gothic church, colorful residences, and attractive shops.

- How to plan an archipelago cruise. You may book an archipelago trip online or at the ferry ports in Portovenere or La Spezia. The official website of the ferry business that handles the boats in Cinque Terre is [Consorzio Marittimo Turistico 5 Terre Golfo dei Poeti]. You may check the schedules, rates, and updates on the boat service there. You may also purchase tickets online or at the ferry docks in each village. The price of an archipelago cruise is 15 euros per person, or 10 euros if you have a Cinque Terre Card.

- When to go on an archipelago cruise. The archipelago cruise runs from April to October, with daily departures from Portovenere and La Spezia. The first departure is at 10:30 a.m. and the final one is at 5:30 p.m. The ideal time to go on an archipelago cruise is in the morning or late afternoon when the light is better for photography and the temperature is more agreeable. You may also enjoy a sunset cruise that leaves at 7:30 p.m. and returns at 9:00 p.m., with a glass of wine provided.

- What to carry on an archipelago cruise. You should pack a hat, sunglasses, sunscreen, water, snacks, and a camera for your archipelago cruise. You should also choose comfortable clothing and shoes that are ideal for walking on difficult terrain. You may also want to bring a jacket or a sweater, since it may be windy or cool on the boat. If you want to stop in Portovenere, you may also want to carry some cash for shopping or dining.

What to see on an archipelago cruise. Here are some of the highlights of what you may see on an archipelago cruise:

- **Palmaria:** This is the biggest and most populated island in the archipelago, with a surface area of approximately 2 square kilometers and a population of around 50 people. It boasts a diversified topography, including rocky cliffs, sandy beaches, caverns, and pine woods. It also has a rich history, including remnants of ancient communities, Roman ruins, Napoleonic defenses, and a former jail. You may view some of these sights from the boat, such as the Grotta Azzurra (Blue Cave), the Torre Scola

(Scola Tower), and the Batteria Umberto I (Umberto I Battery).

- **Tino:** This is a tiny and rocky island that is only accessible once a year, on September 13th, when pilgrims visit its old monastery and cathedral dedicated to Saint Venerius, the patron saint of lighthouse keepers. The island contains a lighthouse that goes back to 1839 and is still in service. It also contains a military cemetery where troops who perished during World War I are buried. You can view these sites from the boat, as well as some of the uncommon flora and wildlife that dwell on the island.

- **Tinetto:** This is the tiniest and most remote island of the archipelago, with a surface area of just 0.08 square kilometers and no permanent residents. It includes a noteworthy archaeological site that consists of a hermitage erected between the 6th and 11th centuries by monks who followed Saint Venerius. The hermitage comprises seven terraces linked by steps cut into the rock, with chapels, chambers, cisterns, and paintings. You may see this location from the boat, as well as some of the aquatic life that surrounds the island.

- **Portovenere:** This is a lovely town that is frequently called the sixth hamlet of Cinque Terre since it has the same natural and cultural legacy. It boasts a lovely port, a historic castle, a Gothic church, colorful residences, and attractive shops. You may explore its sights on foot, or enjoy a panoramic tour of the town from the boat. You may also sample some of its delicacies, like pesto, focaccia, and anchovies.

An archipelago cruise is a superb opportunity to visit the islands of Palmaria, Tino, and Tinetto, as well as the town of Portovenere, which are part of the Cinque Terre UNESCO World Heritage Site. You may appreciate the breathtaking scenery, the rich history, and the unique animals of these islands, and learn more about their culture and customs.

You may also combine the trip with a stop in Portovenere, where you can tour its historic castle, a Gothic church, colorful residences, and attractive shops. An archipelago cruise is a must-do activity for everyone who wishes to enjoy the beauty and charm of Cinque Terre from a new viewpoint.

Winter Activities in Cinque Terre

Cinque Terre is a lovely location on the Italian Riviera, noted for its five colorful towns, spectacular hiking paths, and great food. However, it is not just a summer paradise, but also a winter wonderland, with lots of activities and attractions to enjoy throughout the colder months. Here are some of the greatest winter activities in Cinque Terre for 2023-2024, based on ratings, reviews, and popularity.

Cinque Terre in winter is silent, chilly, and damp. The greatest time to visit Cinque Terre for anybody on a budget is around December and January, save for the holiday season. Some of the best things to see and do in Cinque Terre in winter include touring the five villages by train, hiking excursions, discovering the statue of The Giant in Monterosso al Mare, visiting the National Park, enjoying the Aria Festival of classical music and relaxing over coffee in Riomaggiore's picturesque Piazza Vignaioli. Though winter is typically wet here, some travelers enjoy this season as it's the least popular time of year to come.

Tour the Five Villages by Train

The quickest and fastest way to tour Cinque Terre in winter is by rail. The regional trains operate less often throughout the winter, but no issues are getting between the Cinque Terre settlements. In the off-season, the trains are operating once or twice an hour. You may purchase single rail tickets for roughly 2.50 euros apiece or a day pass for 16 euros that cover unlimited train trips and entry to select museums and sites. You may also enjoy the views of the seaside and the countryside from the train windows.

Hike the Trails

The Cinque Terre hiking routes are available all year round. From November 6 to March 17, all paths are free, and you do not need a Cinque Terre Card. After heavy rain, certain paths might be closed for safety reasons. In this circumstance, there are always alternate paths available. Hiking in winter may be a wonderful experience, as you can appreciate the environment and the vistas without the people and the heat. Some of the greatest paths to trek in winter are:

Levanto - Monterosso: A moderate path that takes approximately 2 hours and gives spectacular views of the sea and the rocks. You may start from either Levanto or Monterosso and follow the signs for SVA (Sentiero Verde Azzurro).

Manarola - Volastra - Corniglia: An easy walk that takes around 1.5 hours and runs through vineyards, olive orchards, and woodlands. You may start at Manarola and take the bus to Volastra or climb up the steps. Then follow the signs for SVA until you reach Corniglia.

Vernazza - Monterosso: A tough walk that takes around 2 hours and travels up and down high slopes and steps. You may start at either Vernazza or Monterosso and follow the signs towards SVA. This hike provides some of the most stunning views of Cinque Terre.

Discover The Giant at Monterosso al Mare

One of the most intriguing things in Cinque Terre is The Giant (Il Gigante), a colossal monument of Neptune that sits on a rock near Fegina Beach in Monterosso al Mare. The monument was erected in 1910 by artist Arrigo Minerbi as part of a home belonging to an English aristocracy. The monument was designed to signify strength and might, but it was badly damaged by bombs during World War II and by storms over the years. Today, just half of the monument survives, yet it nevertheless amazes tourists with its grandeur and history.

Visit the National Park

The Cinque Terre National Park is one of the oldest and smallest national parks in Italy, encompassing an area of around 4,300 hectares. The park preserves not only the natural environment of Cinque Terre, but also its cultural history, such as the terraced vineyards, the dry-stone walls, and the historic settlements. The park provides numerous activities and services for tourists, including guided tours, educational seminars, exhibits, festivals, and more. You may visit the park's headquarters in Riomaggiore or its information centers in each town to discover more about its history, flora, animals, and initiatives.

Enjoy the Aria Festival

The Aria Festival is an annual event that takes place in Cinque Terre from December to January. It is a festival of classical music that comprises performances by local and international performers in different locations throughout the five villages. The event seeks to promote culture and tourism in Cinque Terre, as well as to fund the repair and preservation of its churches and monuments. The festival gives a unique chance to hear high-quality music in a picturesque and historic environment.

Relax over Coffee in Riomaggiore

Riomaggiore is the biggest and busiest of the five settlements, and the one closest to La Spezia. It is a busy and colorful area, with a little port, a pebbly beach, and a high slope. One of the nicest things to do in Riomaggiore in winter is to relax over a cup of coffee in one of its cafes and enjoy the view of the hamlet and the sea. You may select from several alternatives, such as Bar Centrale, Bar O'Netto, or Bar e Vini a Piè de Mà. You may also taste some local sweets, such as focaccia or cannoli, or some local wines, such as Cinque Terre DOC or Sciacchetrà.

These are just some of the greatest winter activities in Cinque Terre for 2023-2024. For additional information and inspiration, you may check out these websites:

Cinque Terre is a beautiful site to visit in winter since it provides a different and more real experience than in summer. You may enjoy the beauty and the charm of the five villages without the crowds and the heat, and discover some hidden jewels and attractions that are available all year round. You may also take advantage of the reduced costs and the free trails, and immerse yourself in the local culture and food. Whether you're searching for adventure, leisure, or romance, Cinque Terre provides something for everyone in winter. So don't delay and book your vacation to Cinque Terre immediately!

CHAPTER 7

SURROUNDING AREAS OF CINQUE TERRE

Cinque Terre is a lovely location on the Italian Riviera, noted for its five colorful towns, spectacular hiking paths, and great food. However, it is not the only location worth visiting in this area, since there are many other cities and attractions around that provide diverse experiences and viewpoints. Here are some of the greatest neighboring locations of Cinque Terre for 2023-2024, based on ratings, reviews, and popularity.

Cinque Terre is situated on the coastline of northern Italy, in what is known as the Italian Riviera: a small coastal strip between the South of France's Cote d'Azur and Tuscany. What makes this location so distinctive is how its settlements are bordered by the stunning deep blue sea on one side and backed by the rugged Maritime Alps on the other.

Levanto

Levanto is a lovely hamlet located just north of Cinque Terre and is frequently called the sixth village in the region. It is a popular base for touring Cinque Terre since it has a railway station that links to all five towns, as well as a boat service that operates from April to October. Levanto boasts a long sandy beach that draws surfers and sunbathers, as well as a historic town that contains a medieval castle, a Gothic church, and a vibrant market. Levanto is also a fantastic site for trekking since it has various routes that go to Cinque Terre or other local villages.

Portovenere

Portovenere is a scenic town that sits south of Cinque Terre and is part of the UNESCO World Heritage Site along with the five towns. It is a magnificent destination to visit, with its colorful buildings, its medieval castle, its Romanesque church, and its natural caverns. Portovenere also has a small port that allows boat cruises to Cinque Terre or the adjacent islands of Palmaria, Tino, and Tinetto. Portovenere is noted for its seafood cuisine, notably its mussels, and anchovies.

La Spezia

La Spezia is a big city that sits east of Cinque Terre and is the primary transit center for the region. It features a railroad station that links to all five settlements, as well as an airport that services local and international flights. La

Spezia is not extremely touristic, but it has several intriguing sights to offer, such as its naval museum, its art museum, its castle, and its market. La Spezia is also a fantastic spot to buy local items, such as wine, olive oil, pesto, cheese, and honey.

Sarzana

Sarzana is a little village located inland from Cinque Terre and is approximately 40 minutes distant by rail. It is a wonderful site to visit, with its medieval walls, its Gothic cathedral, its Renaissance palaces, and its antique stores. Sarzana has a rich cultural legacy since it was the birthplace of various writers and painters. Sarzana also holds certain festivals and events throughout the year, such as the Soffitta nella Strada (an antique market) in August and the Aria Festival (a classical music festival) in December.

Chiavari

Chiavari is a charming town located north of Cinque Terre and is roughly an hour distant by rail. It is an affluent place with some spectacular buildings, such as its arcades, its churches, and its villas. Chiavari features a vibrant retail center with several stores and cafés, as well as a market that takes place every Friday. Chiavari also boasts a lengthy beach that provides numerous water sports and activities.

Cinque Terre is a beautiful site to visit, but it is not the only one in this area. There are many more towns and sites around that provide various experiences and viewpoints. You may tour the picturesque towns of Levanto, Portovenere, La Spezia, Sarzana, and Chiavari, and learn about their history, culture, gastronomy, and environment. You may also enjoy the sea, the mountains, the wineries, and the markets that make this place so wonderful. Whether you're seeking adventure, leisure, or romance, you'll find something for everyone in the surrounding regions of Cinque Terre. So don't delay and plan your vacation to Cinque Terre and its neighbors immediately! You won't regret it!

CHAPTER 8

7-Days Itinerary in Cinque Terre

Cinque Terre, the five lovely towns on the Ligurian coast, is a wonderful location for those who appreciate nature, culture, and gastronomy. The area provides breathtaking landscapes, colorful residences, historic churches, fascinating shops, and wonderful food. You may tour the villages by rail, boat, or foot, and enjoy the views of the sea and the hills. Here is a proposed plan for 7 days in Cinque Terre, based on the greatest sites and activities in each hamlet.

Day 1: Arrive in Pisa and Transfer to Monterosso al Mare

Your tour begins in Pisa, where you may fly into the international airport and take a train or private transport to Monterosso al Mare, the biggest and most developed hamlet in Cinque Terre. Monterosso boasts a large sandy beach, a busy promenade, and a historic town with a castle and a church. You may check into your hotel and rest for a bit, then go out to tour the town. You may wander along the beach and enjoy the sun and the water, or explore the medieval tower of Aurora that formerly defended the town from pirates. You may also witness the statue of the Giant, a 14-meter-high monument that symbolizes Neptune grasping a shell-shaped terrace. For supper, you may taste some of the local favorites such as anchovies, pesto pasta, and seafood risotto.

Day 2: Visit Riomaggiore and Manarola

Visit two of the other communities in Cinque Terre: Riomaggiore and Manarola. You may take a train from Monterosso to Riomaggiore, the southernmost settlement in the area. Riomaggiore includes a gorgeous port with colorful boats and residences, a castle with panoramic views, and a church with a marble front. You may wander about the town and appreciate its beauty, or go up to the sanctuary of Madonna di Montenero, where you can enjoy a spectacular view of the coast. You may also visit the local museum that showcases objects and images relating to the history and culture of Cinque Terre. For lunch, you may sample some of the local foods such as farinata (a chickpea flour pancake) or focaccia (a flatbread with varied toppings).

In the afternoon, you may take a short train journey or walk down the famed route called Via dell'Amore (Lovers' Walk) to Manarola, the second smallest hamlet in Cinque Terre. Manarola is recognized for its gorgeous setting on a rocky peninsula, its colorful buildings that fall to the sea, and its vines that create a sweet wine called Sciacchetrà. You may tour the town and view its key features such as the church of San Lorenzo, the bell tower that was formerly a watchtower, and the nativity scene that is lit at night. You may also take a boat trip or hire a kayak to observe the shore from a different angle. For supper, you may savor some of the excellent seafood that Manarola is famed for.

Day 3: Visit Corniglia and Vernazza

You will visit two additional villages in Cinque Terre: Corniglia and Vernazza. You may take a train from Manarola to Corniglia, the smallest and tallest settlement in the area. Corniglia is built on top of a hill surrounded by vineyards and olive trees, and it has a more rural and tranquil character than the other settlements. You may access the town by ascending 377 stairs or catching a shuttle bus from the railway station. You may wander about the town and visit its key sights such as the church of San

Pietro, the terrace of Santa Maria Belvedere, and the remnants of Genoese defenses. You may also drink some of the local wine at one of the numerous taverns or vineyards in town.

In the afternoon, you may take a train or stroll along a gorgeous route to Vernazza, one of the most stunning settlements in Cinque Terre. Vernazza boasts a picturesque port with colorful boats and residences, a castle with an observation tower, and a church with an octagonal tower that overlooks the sea. You may visit the town and view its key sights like the church of Santa Margherita d'Antiochia, the Doria Castle, and the Belforte Tower. You may also relax on the little beach or take a boat excursion to view some of the secret coves along the coast. For supper, you may taste some of the local delicacies such as trofie al pesto (twisted pasta with basil sauce) or stuffed mussels.

Day 4: Free Day in Cinque Terre

You have a free day to discover Cinque Terre at your leisure. You might opt to return to some of the communities that you enjoyed the best or experience some of the other sights and activities that the area provides. Here are some possibilities for your free day:

- Hike along the pathways that link the settlements and enjoy the views of the sea and the hills. You may pick from numerous degrees of difficulty and duration, based on your desire and fitness level. Some of the more popular paths include the Sentiero Azzurro (Blue Trail) which goes along the coast, the Sentiero Rosso (Red Trail) which climbs the mountains, and the Sentiero Verde (Green Trail) which travels through the vineyards and woodlands.

- Snorkel or scuba dive in the clean and lush waters of Cinque Terre, where you may view diverse marine animals such as octopus, moray eels, groupers, and lobsters. You may hire equipment and explore on your own, or join a guided trip that will take you to the greatest sites and show you the marine richness of Cinque Terre. Some of the most popular diving sites include Il Gabbiano, La Grotta dei Gamberi, and Il Relitto del Tino.

- Visit some of the adjacent towns or cities that are worth a day trip from Cinque Terre, such as Portovenere, Lerici, La Spezia, or Pisa. You may take a train or a boat to visit these sites and experience their attractions and atmosphere. Portovenere is a lovely village with a castle, a cathedral, and a grotto that inspired authors like Byron and Shelley. Lerici is a coastal resort comprising a castle, a beach, and a marina. La Spezia is a city featuring a naval museum, a contemporary art museum, and a vibrant market. Pisa is a city featuring a renowned leaning tower, a church, and a baptistery.

Day 5: Transfer to Portofino and Enjoy a Sunset Kayak Tour

Today you will leave Cinque Terre and go to Portofino, another magnificent village on the Ligurian coast. Portofino is an attractive and exclusive resort that draws celebrities and jet-setters from all over the globe. It boasts a gorgeous port with luxury boats and colorful buildings, a castle with a museum and a park, and a church with a lighthouse. You may check into your hotel and rest for a bit, then go out to tour the town. You may wander around the port and appreciate the views of the sea and the hills, or visit some of the prominent sights such as the church of San Giorgio, the castle of Brown, and the park of Portofino.

In the evening, you may enjoy a sunset kayak excursion that will take you around the coast of Portofino and show you its beauty from a fresh viewpoint. You may paddle along the rocky beach, enjoying the colorful buildings of Portofino from a distance, or explore some of the secret coves and caves that dot the coast. You may also observe some of the marine species that inhabit these seas, such as fish, crabs, starfish, and seagulls. You may stop for a swim or a snack at one of the peaceful areas along the road, or simply relax and enjoy the sunset over the sea.

Day 6: Enjoy a Boat Tour of San Fruttuoso Abbey

Today you will experience a boat journey that will take you to San Fruttuoso Abbey, one of the most intriguing destinations on the Ligurian coast. San Fruttuoso Abbey is a historic monastery that goes back to the 10th century and is set in a quiet cove surrounded by pine trees and rocks. The abbey comprises a Romanesque church, a cloister, a tower, and various chapels. It also holds an underwater statue of

Christ named Christ of the Abyss which was installed in 1954 to protect divers and fishermen. You may tour the abbey and learn more about its history and architecture, or swim or scuba dive to view the statue and other underwater sights.

After seeing San Fruttuoso Abbey, you may continue your boat journey to Camogli, another picturesque village on the Ligurian coast. Camogli is noted for its fishing culture, its colorful buildings that line up along the coastal promenade, and its basilica that overlooks the port. You may go about Camogli and explore its key sights such as the cathedral of Santa Maria Assunta, the castle of Dragonara, and the museum of marine culture. You may also enjoy some of Camogli's specialties such as focaccia al formaggio (cheese-filled flatbread) or frittelle di baccalà (cod fritters).

Day 7: Departure

Today your vacation comes to an end. You may have your final breakfast in Portofino before checking out from your hotel and traveling to the airport for your trip home. You may take a train or private transport to Genoa or Pisa, where you can catch your flight. Alternatively, you may prolong your vacation and visit some of the other locations in Italy, such as Florence, Rome, Venice, or Naples. You will depart with memorable recollections of Cinque Terre and its natural and cultural treasures.

Cinque Terre is a location that will fascinate you with its beauty, charm, and variety. In 7 days, you may tour each of the five villages and its attractions, as well as some of the adjacent towns and cities that are worth a visit. You may also enjoy several outdoor activities, like hiking, kayaking, snorkeling, and paragliding, that will enable you to explore Cinque Terre from other views. You may also taste the local food, wine, and culture, that highlight the rich and genuine legacy of this region. Cinque Terre is a destination where you may relax, have fun, and discover something new every day.

CHAPTER 9

PRACTICAL INFORMATION AND TIPS FOR CINQUE TERRE

Etiquette and traditions

Cinque Terre is an area of Italy that has a rich and varied history, culture, and character. The people who live in the five villages are proud of their legacy and traditions, and they want tourists to respect them and their way of life. To assist you avoid any misunderstandings or faux pas, here are some ideas and guidance on how to behave and interact with the people in Cinque Terre.

Greetings and introductions

When you meet someone for the first time in Cinque Terre, you should welcome them with a handshake and a grin. You should also say "buongiorno" (good morning) or "Buona sera" (good evening), depending on the time of day. If you know the individual well, or if they are a friend or a family, you may also kiss them on both cheeks.

You should also identify yourself with your name and your nationality, and ask them their name and where they are from. You may use the formal "lei" (you) or the casual "tu" (you) to address them, depending on the circumstances and the connection. In general, you should use the formal "lei" with strangers, seniors, professionals, or authorities, and the casual "tu" with friends, peers, or children.

You should also be aware of various common titles and honorifics that are used in Cinque Terre, such as:

- Signore (Mr.) or Signora (Mrs.) for married or elderly folks
- Signorina (Miss) for unmarried or younger ladies
- Dottore (Doctor) or Professor (Professor) for those with academic degrees or occupations
- Don (Father) or Suora (Sister) for priests or nuns
- Sindaco (Mayor) or Assessore (Councilor) for local officials

You should always use these titles followed by the surname of the individual unless they encourage you to use their name.

Conversation and communication

When you have a chat with someone in Cinque Terre, you should be courteous, kind, and considerate. You should also be attentive, inquisitive, and interested in what they have to say. You may ask them questions about their lives, their family, their career, or their interests, but avoid issues that may be sensitive or contentious, such as politics, religion, or money.

You should also be aware of several cultural variations and subtleties that may affect your conversation in Cinque Terre, such as:

- **Body language:** Italians are expressive and lively when they communicate, and they utilize a lot of gestures and facial expressions to convey their feelings and thoughts. You should not be scared or angered by this, but rather strive to grasp their intention and react properly. You should also avoid gestures that may be unpleasant or disrespectful in Italy, such as pointing your finger, touching your nose, or making the "OK" sign.

- **Eye contact:** Italians keep eye contact while they converse, as a gesture of respect and attention. You should do the same, but not gaze too much or too fiercely, since it may be perceived as hostile or invasive.

- **Personal space:** Italians like to stand near to each other while they converse, as a display of warmth and closeness. You should not back away or create too much space, since it may be perceived as cold or unfriendly. However, you should also respect their personal space and not touch them too much or too frequently, unless they initiate it.

- **Humor:** Italians have a fantastic sense of humor and they enjoy laughing and teasing each other. You should not take everything they say literally or seriously, but rather engage in the fun and laugh along. However, you should also be cautious not to make jokes that may be unsuitable or insulting in Italy, such as jokes about religion or stereotypes.

Dining and drinking

When you eat or drink in Cinque Terre, you should respect certain fundamental norms of etiquette and traditions that are typical in Italy. Here are some of them:

- **Timing:** Italians have distinct eating hours from most other nations. They normally consume breakfast between 7 am and 9 am, lunch between 12 pm and 2 pm, and supper between 8 pm and 10 pm. They also enjoy a snack called Merenda between 4 pm and 6 pm. You should attempt to adjust to these schedules when you dine out in Cinque Terre since most restaurants follow them.

- **Ordering:** Italians normally order from a menu that is separated into many courses: antipasti (appetizers), primi (first meals, usually pasta or soup), second (second courses, usually meat or fish), contorni (side dishes, usually vegetables or salad), dolci (desserts) and caffè (coffee). You don't have to purchase all the courses, but you should order at least one from each category. You should also order water and wine to complement your meal and ask for the bill after you're done.

- **Tipping:** Tipping is not necessary in Italy, since most restaurants include a service fee in the bill. However, it's normal to give a little tip of roughly 10% of the bill or round up to the closest euro, if you're delighted with the service and the quality of the cuisine. You should also tip the waiter immediately and not leave it on the table.

- **Drinking:** Italians like drinking wine, beer, and spirits, but they do it sparingly and responsibly. They normally drink wine with their meals, beer with their snacks, and spirits as a digestif after their meals. They also drink coffee throughout the day, however, they normally drink espresso or cappuccino, and never after supper. You should follow their example and drink carefully and properly in Cinque Terre.

Dressing and shopping

When you dress or purchase in Cinque Terre, you should be aware of the basic manners and traditions that are prevalent in Italy. Here are some of them:

- **Dressing:** Italians are elegant and fashionable, and they devote attention to their looks and their attire. You should do the same, and dress correctly and politely for the event and the area. You should avoid wearing shorts, flip-flops, tank tops, or caps in churches or museums, since they may be deemed impolite or unsuitable. You should also avoid wearing overly exposing or too casual clothing at restaurants or pubs, since they may be deemed unpleasant or obscene.

- **Shopping:** Italians adore shopping, and they have a lot of stores and marketplaces that offer different items and products. You should enjoy exploring and purchasing in Cinque Terre, but you should also be nice and courteous with the merchants and the consumers. You should always greet the vendor with a "buongiorno" or a "Buona sera", ask for permission before touching or testing anything, and thank them with a "Grazie" before you leave. You should also haggle nicely and moderately if the price is not set or if you purchase more than one thing.

Language and communication in Cinque Terre

Cinque Terre is a region in Italy, where the official language is Italian. However, you may also meet several local dialects and languages that are peculiar to this region, such as Ligurian, Genoese, and Cinque Terre's vernacular. Here is a draft of the chapter that I have prepared based on the online search results.

- How to converse in Cinque Terre. If you wish to connect with the people in Cinque Terre, you need to learn some basic Italian phrases and vocabulary, since not everyone speaks English or other foreign languages. You may utilize online resources such as [Duolingo] or [Babbel] to learn some Italian before your trip or purchase a phrasebook or a dictionary to aid you throughout your stay. You may also download several applications such as [Google Translate] or [Microsoft Translator] to translate words or phrases on your phone. However, you should also be aware of various distinctions and subtleties between standard Italian and the local dialects and languages of Cinque Terre, such as pronunciation, vocabulary, syntax, and idioms. Here are some instances of these differences:

- **Pronunciation:** The inhabitants of Cinque Terre prefer to lose the last vowels of words, particularly when they talk swiftly or informally. For example, "buongiorno" (good morning) may sound like "Buon Giorno", "Grazie" (thank you) may sound like "graze", and "arrivederci" (goodbye) may sound like "arrivederci".

- **Vocabulary:** The residents in Cinque Terre use several terms that are distinct from standard Italian, either because they are derived from Ligurian or Genoese, or because they are peculiar to the culture and landscape of Cinque Terre. For example, "focaccia" (a kind of bread) is called "fugassa", "pesto" (a sauce consisting of basil, garlic, pine nuts, cheese, and oil) is called "pestu", and "sciacchetrà" (a sweet wine made of dried grapes) is called "sciachetrà".

- **Grammar:** The residents in Cinque Terre utilize various grammatical constructions that are distinct from normal Italian, either because they are influenced by Ligurian or Genoese, or because they are simplified or abbreviated variants of regular Italian. For example, "ci sono" (there are) is frequently substituted by "ghe son", "non c'è" (there is not) is often replaced by "n'è", and "mi piace" (I enjoy) is sometimes replaced by "me piase".

- **Idioms:** The residents in Cinque Terre employ various idioms and phrases that are unique to this region, either because they represent the lifestyle and attitude of the people, or because they are tied to the history and legends of Cinque Terre. For example, "fare il gatto e la volpe" (to act like the cat and the fox) means to be cunning and dishonest, "essere come il prezzemolo" (to be like parsley) means to be everywhere or involved in everything, and "andare a zonzo" (to go wandering) means to explore or enjoy Cinque Terre without a specific destination.

- How to be courteous and considerate in Cinque Terre. If you wish to be nice and respectful in Cinque Terre, you need to observe certain fundamental norms of etiquette and manners that are customary throughout Italy and in this area. Here are some ideas to help you be nice and considerate in Cinque Terre:

- Greet individuals with a grin and a handshake, even a kiss on both cheeks if you know them well. Use formal titles such as "signore" (sir), "signora" (madam), or "signorina" (miss) unless you are encouraged to use first names.

- Say "buongiorno" (good morning) until noon, "buon pomeriggio" (good afternoon) until 6 p.m., and "buona sera" (good evening) after 6 p.m. Say "buona notte" (good night) just when you are leaving or going to bed.

- Say "per favore" (please), "Grazie" (thank you), "prego" (you're welcome), "scusi" (excuse me), and "mi dispiace" (I'm sorry) when appropriate. These words indicate respect and decency.

- Dress properly for the event and the venue. Avoid wearing shorts, flip-flops, tank tops, or caps at churches or other religious institutions. Cover your shoulders and knees before entering these regions. Wear suitable shoes and attire for hiking or walking on the trails. Avoid wearing bright or costly jewelry or accessories that may draw unwelcome attention.

- Respect the nature and the culture of Cinque Terre. Don't trash or leave any traces behind. Don't pluck flowers or fruits. Don't feed or disturb animals. Don't make loud sounds or play music. Don't trespass or jump over fences. Don't take photographs or films of individuals without their consent. Don't touch or damage any artwork or monuments.

language and communication in Cinque Terre is a crucial component of your journey that may boost your comprehension and admiration of this place. You should acquire some fundamental Italian phrases and vocabulary, as well as some of the local dialects and languages that are peculiar to Cinque Terre. You should also respect certain fundamental standards of etiquette and politeness that are popular in Italy and this area. By doing so, you may connect with the locals courteously and pleasantly, and learn more about their culture and customs. Language and communication in Cinque Terre is not only functional skill but also a method to connect with the people and the area.

Simple Words and Terms to Know in Cinque Terre

Cinque Terre is a picturesque location on the Italian Riviera, noted for its five colorful towns, spectacular hiking paths, and great food. However, it is also a location with its own culture, history, and language, and learning some fundamental phrases and terminology will help you make the most of your stay there. Here are some of the most helpful words and keywords to know in Cinque Terre for 2023-2024, based on ratings, reviews, and popularity.

Cinque Terre means "Five Lands" in Italian, and refers to the five communities that make up the area: Monterosso al Mare, Vernazza, Corniglia, Manarola, and Riomaggiore. Each hamlet has its charm and individuality, and you may explore them by rail, boat, or foot.

Greetings and Basic Phrases

The official language of Cinque Terre is Italian, although the residents also speak a dialect called Ligurian or Ligure. Ligurian is a Romance language that has some parallels with French and Spanish, but also notable deviations from standard Italian. You don't need to learn Ligurian to visit Cinque Terre, although you may hear certain terms or idioms that are peculiar to the region. Here are some greetings and simple words in both Italian and Ligurian that will help you converse with the locals:

- Hello: Ciao (Italian) / Aiva (Ligurian)
- Good morning: Buongiorno (Italian) / Bon dì (Ligurian)
- Good evening: Buonasera (Italian) / Bona sera (Ligurian)
- Good night: Buonanotte (Italian) / Bona note (Ligurian)
- Goodbye: Arrivederci (Italian) / A revéde (Ligurian)
- Thank you: Grazie (Italian) / Grassie (Ligurian)
- You're welcome: Prego (Italian) / Prego or De niente (Ligurian)
- Excuse me: Scusi (Italian) / Scuxeme or Scusèime (Ligurian)
- I'm sorry: Mi dispiace (Italian) / Me dispiase or Me spiase (Ligurian)
- Yes: Sì (Italian) / Sì or Sciù (Ligurian)
- No: No (Italian) / No or Nòn (Ligurian)

Food and Drink

One of the nicest things about visiting Cinque Terre is savoring its cuisine and wine. The cuisine of Cinque Terre is centered on the native products of the land and the sea, such as olives, grapes, basil, anchovies, mussels, and tuna. The recipes are simple and healthful, cooked with extra virgin olive oil, fresh veggies, herbs, and cheese. Some of the traditional foods you may enjoy in Cinque Terre are:

- Trofie al pesto: Fresh pasta with basil sauce
- Muscoli: Mussels sautéed in white wine and garlic
- Acciughe: Anchovies served in different ways
- Focaccia: Flatbread with olive oil and salt
- Farinata: Flatbread prepared from chickpea flour
- Sciacchetrà: A sweet wine produced from dried grapes

Here are some words and phrases connected to food and drink in both Italian and Ligurian that might assist you order at a restaurant or a bar:

- Menu: Menù (Italian) / Menù or Carta (Ligurian)
- Bill: Conto (Italian) / Conto or Cònta (Ligurian)

172

- Water: Acqua (Italian) / Aqua or Euga (Ligurian)
- Wine: Vino (Italian) / Vin or Vinn-a (Ligurian)
- Beer: Birra (Italian) / Birra or Bira (Ligurian)
- Coffee: Caffè (Italian) / Caffè or Cafèu (Ligurian)
- Tea: Tè (Italian) / Tè or Teu (Ligurian)

- Bread: Pane (Italian) / Pan or Pann-a (Ligurian)
- Cheese: Formaggio (Italian) / Formaggio or Formagg-iu (Ligurian)
- Fish: Pesce (Italian) / Pesce or Pesc-eu (Ligurian)

Places and Directions

Another fantastic part about visiting Cinque Terre is discovering its locations and attractions. The region has a lot to offer, from its lovely villages to its natural park to its adjacent cities. You may see the churches, the castles, the museums, the beaches, and the marketplaces that make Cinque Terre so wonderful. You may also trek the trails, take a boat ride, or hire a bike to view more of the shore and the countryside.

Here are some words and concepts relating to locations and routes in both Italian and Ligurian that will help you find your way to Cinque Terre:

- Village: Paese (Italian) / Paese or Pais-eu (Ligurian)
- Church: Chiesa (Italian) / Chiesa or Cies-a (Ligurian)
- Castle: Castello (Italian) / Castello or Castell-u (Ligurian)
- Museum: Museo (Italian) / Museo or Museu (Ligurian)
- Beach: Spiaggia (Italian) / Spiaggia or Spiaza (Ligurian)
- Market: Mercato (Italian) / Mercato or Mercàu (Ligurian)
- Train: Treno (Italian) / Treno or Tren-u (Ligurian)
- Boat: Barca (Italian) / Barca or Barch-a (Ligurian)
- Bike: Bicicletta (Italian) / Bicicletta or Biciclett-a (Ligurian)
- Left: Sinistra (Italian) / Sinistra or Sinistr-a (Ligurian)
- Right: Destra (Italian) / Destra or Destr-a (Ligurian)
- Straight: Dritto (Italian) / Dritto or Drìtt-u (Ligurian)

Cinque Terre is a gorgeous site to visit, but it is also a region with its own culture, history, and language. Knowing some easy phrases and terminology will help you converse with the people, order at a restaurant or a bar, and make your way around the neighborhood. You don't need to be proficient in Italian or Ligurian, but learning some fundamental words and expressions will make your vacation more pleasurable and memorable. So don't delay and start learning some phrases and terminology to know in Cinque Terre immediately! You'll be astonished at how much you can learn and how much fun you can have!

Health and Safety Tips in Cinque Terre

Cinque Terre, the five charming towns on the Ligurian coast, is a superb location for tourists who wish to appreciate nature, culture, and gastronomy. The location is typically secure and serene, but there are certain health and safety considerations that you should bear in mind to make your vacation more pleasurable and hassle-free. Here are some of the most critical health and safety considerations in Cinque Terre:

1. Be prepared for hiking

One of the primary attractions of Cinque Terre is trekking along the paths that link the towns and give amazing views of the sea and the hills. However, hiking in Cinque Terre is hardly a stroll in the park. The routes may be steep, rocky, narrow, and treacherous, particularly after rain. You need to wear adequate footwear, such as hiking boots or shoes, and avoid flip-flops or heels. You also need to pack extra water, sunscreen, a hat, sunglasses, and snacks, since there are not many amenities along the road. You should also check the weather forecast and the trail conditions before you travel, since certain routes may be blocked due to landslides or repairs. You may get current information on the official website of Cinque Terre National Park.

2. Be cautious while swimming

Cinque Terre offers several wonderful beaches and coves where you may swim and relax in the crystal blue ocean. However, you need also to be cautious while swimming in Cinque Terre, since there are several dangers and risks that you should be aware of. First of all, most of the beaches are stony or pebbly, therefore you should wear water shoes or sandals to protect your feet from cuts and accidents. Second, some of the beaches feature strong currents or waves that may make swimming difficult or hazardous, particularly for youngsters or new swimmers. You should always obey the signs and flags that indicate the swimming conditions and observe the lifeguards' directions. Third, some of the beaches include jellyfish or sea urchins that may sting or harm you if you contact them. You should avoid swimming near them or wear a wetsuit or rash guard to protect your skin.

3. Be considerate to the locals

Cinque Terre is a prominent tourist area that draws millions of people every year. However, it is also a living and working area for the natives who have been living there for ages. The residents are nice and welcoming, but they also demand respect and regard from the visitors that visit their communities. You should respect their culture, traditions, and practices, such as clothing correctly while visiting churches or monuments, speaking gently when strolling in residential areas, disposing of your waste properly, and not snapping photographs of people without their permission. You should also support their economy by purchasing local items and services, such as wine, cuisine, souvenirs, or excursions.

4. Be wary of small crime

Cinque Terre is a safe area to visit in terms of violent crime, which is relatively unusual in this region. However, small crimes like pickpocketing or scamming may still happen, particularly during peak tourist season when there are big crowds and diversions. You should be watchful and careful while going to Cinque Terre and take certain steps to prevent being a victim of petty crime. You should put your valuables such as money, credit cards, passport, or phone in a secure area such as a hotel safe or a concealed pocket. You should also carry a photocopy of your passport and other crucial papers in case you lose them or they are stolen. You should avoid carrying big sums of cash or wearing bright items that might draw attention. You should also be aware of people who approach you with offers or demands that appear too good to be true or suspicious.

5. Be prepared for crises

Cinque Terre is a well-equipped and well-connected location that offers all the required services and amenities for visitors. However, crises may still happen anytime and anyplace, so you should be prepared for them in case they do. You should have travel insurance that covers medical expenditures, theft, loss, or cancellation in case anything goes wrong during your vacation. You should also have some emergency contacts that you may phone or reach if you need support or assistance. Here are some of the most critical emergency contacts in Cinque Terre:

- Emergency number: 112 (for police, fire brigade, ambulance)
- Cinque Terre National Park: +39 0187 762600 (for information on trails and activities)

- Tourist office: +39 0187 920633 (for information on accommodation and activities)
- Consulate: +39 06 46741 (for information on visas and passports)

Cinque Terre is a location that will fascinate you with its beauty, charm, and variety. However, to make your vacation more fun and hassle-free, you should also follow basic health and safety advice that will help you avoid difficulties and hazards. By being prepared, attentive, courteous, alert, and prepared, you can make the most of your time in Cinque Terre and have a wonderful and safe vacation.

Emergency contacts

Cinque Terre is a safe and serene area of Italy, where you may spend a calm and unforgettable holiday. However, accidents and emergencies may happen anywhere and anytime, and you should be prepared and aware in case you need aid or assistance. In this chapter, we'll present you with some important information and contacts for emergency circumstances in Cinque Terre, such as medical, police, fire, or consular services.

Emergency numbers

The first thing you should know is how to contact emergency services in Italy. The general emergency number is 112, which links you to the Carabinieri, the national military police force. They can help you with any form of emergency, such as crime, violence, terrorism, or natural catastrophes. They may also transmit your call to other emergency services, such as ambulance, fire brigade, or coast guard.

However, you may also contact the individual emergency numbers for each agency, if you prefer or if you know what sort of aid you need. Here are the primary emergency numbers in Italy:

- **113:** Polizia di Stato (State Police), the national civil police agency. They can aid you with crime prevention, public order, traffic management, and immigration difficulties.

- **118:** Servizio Sanitario Nazionale (National Health Service), the national public health system. They can aid you with medical situations, such as accidents, diseases, or poisoning.

- **115:** Vigili del Fuoco (Fire Brigade), the national fire and rescue agency. They can help you with fire situations, such as flames, explosions, or gas leaks.

- **1530:** Guardia Costiera (Coast Guard), the national marine agency. They can aid you with marine emergencies, such as boat accidents, drownings, or pollution.

You should always have these numbers stored on your phone or written down someplace accessible, in case you need to contact them immediately. You should also know how to communicate properly and efficiently when you contact them, by stating your name, location, situation, and requirements.

Medical services

If you require medical care or treatment in Cinque Terre, you have various alternatives to select from. Here are some of them:

- Pharmacies: Pharmacies are the simplest and cheapest method to acquire basic medical treatment in Cinque Terre. They may supply you with over-the-counter drugs, such as painkillers, antihistamines, or antibiotics. They may also advise you on minor problems, such as headaches, colds, or allergies. You may distinguish pharmacies by their green cross sign outside their establishments. They are normally open from Monday to Saturday, from 8 am to 8 pm. However, some of them may shut down for lunch or on Sundays.

- **Doctors:** Doctors are the greatest choice if you require more specialized or severe medical treatment in Cinque Terre. They may detect and treat numerous diseases and disorders, such as infections, fractures, or chronic illnesses. They may also prescribe drugs or refer you to other health experts or institutions. You may find physicians at private clinics or governmental hospitals in Cinque Terre. However, you may need to book an appointment or pay a charge to visit them.

- **Hospitals:** Hospitals are the final choice if you require urgent or life-threatening medical treatment in Cinque Terre. They may give you emergency services, such as surgery, critical care, or trauma treatment. They may also admit you for an overnight stay or longer-term therapy. You may locate hospitals in bigger towns or cities around Cinque Terre, such as La Spezia or Levanto. However, you may have to wait for a long period or pay a significant premium to access them.

You should always bring your travel insurance and health documentation with you when you visit any medical service in Cinque Terre, since they may ask for these before treating you. You should also verify whether your insurance covers the price of the medical service you use, or if you have to pay out of cash.

Police services

If you need police aid or security in Cinque Terre, you have various choices to select from. Here are some of them:

- **Carabinieri:** Carabinieri is the official military police force in Italy. They can help you with any form of emergency event, such as crime, violence, terrorism, or natural catastrophes. They may also offer security and law enforcement services, such as patrolling, investigating, or arresting. You may locate Carabinieri stations in every hamlet in Cinque Terre, or phone them at 112.

- **Polizia di Stato:** Polizia di Stato are the national civil police force of Italy. They can aid you with crime prevention, public order, traffic management, and immigration difficulties. They may also perform administrative and judicial services, such as issuing paperwork, reporting crimes, or testifying in court. You may locate Polizia di Stato stations in bigger towns or cities around Cinque Terre, like La Spezia or Levanto, or phone them at 113.

- **Guardia di Finanza:** Guardia di Finanza is the national financial police force of Italy. They may help you with economic and financial crimes, such as tax evasion, money laundering, or fraud. They may also perform customs and border control services, such as examining goods, vehicles, or persons. You may locate Guardia di Finanza stations in bigger towns or cities around Cinque Terre, like La Spezia or Levanto, or phone them at 117. You can discover a list of Guardia di Finanza stations around Cinque Terre.

You should always carry your passport and visa with you when you visit any police agency in Cinque Terre, since they may ask for them before assisting you. You should also collaborate and comply with their demands and directions since they have the power and the obligation to enforce the law.

Consular services

If you require diplomatic help or protection in Cinque Terre, you have to contact your embassy or consulate in Italy. They may help you with numerous difficulties, such as lost or stolen passports, legal concerns, and medical emergencies. They may also offer consular protection services, such as providing papers, registering citizens, or supporting victims of crime.

You should always carry your embassy or consulate's contact information with you when you go to Cinque Terre, since they may be your sole source of support in case of danger. You should also register with them before or during your journey, so they can contact you or find you in case of an emergency.

I would like to remind you that Cinque Terre is a safe and tranquil area of Italy, where you may spend a calm and unforgettable holiday. However, accidents and emergencies may happen anywhere and anytime, and you should be prepared and aware in case you need aid or assistance.

Internet Access in Cinque Terre

- How to access the internet in Cinque Terre. If you want to use the internet in Cinque Terre, you have numerous possibilities, depending on your requirements and tastes. You may utilize free Wi-Fi hotspots, purchase a local SIM card with an internet connection, or use your own mobile data plan with roaming costs. Here are some ideas and tools to help you access the internet in Cinque Terre:

- Free Wi-Fi hotspots: You may discover free Wi-Fi hotspots in many locations in Cinque Terre, including hotels, restaurants, bars, cafés, stores, railway stations, tourist offices, and public squares. You may need to register with your email address or phone number to utilize them. You may also utilize the free Wi-Fi connection offered by the Cinque Terre National Park if you have a Cinque Terre Card. However, you should be warned that the free Wi-Fi hotspots may not be particularly dependable or fast, especially during busy hours or in rural places.

- Local SIM card with data connection: You may purchase a local SIM card with data connection at any phone shop or electronics authorized dealer in Italy. You may locate them at airports or in locations around Cinque Terre, such as La Spezia. There are no SIM card vendors in Cinque Terre itself. The major Italian carriers are Tim (Telecom Italia Mobile), Vodafone, and Wind Tre. Other operators include Iliad, Ho Mobile, and Kena Mobile. You may compare their plans and costs online or ask for guidance at the shop. You may need to produce your passport or ID card to acquire a SIM card. You may also top up your credit online or at any shop showing the provider emblem. A local SIM card with a data connection may provide you with quick and dependable internet access, as well as cheaper calls and messages throughout Italy.

- Mobile data plan with roaming costs: You may use your own mobile data plan with roaming charges if you have an international or European plan that includes Italy. You should check with your operator about the roaming rates and coverage in Italy before you leave, since they may vary based on your plan and provider. You should also switch off your data roaming when you are not using it, to prevent unnecessary costs. A mobile data plan with roaming costs may provide you convenience and flexibility, but it may also be quite costly or restricted in terms of data consumption.

To summarise, communication and internet connectivity in Cinque Terre is a crucial component of your journey that may help you remain connected and informed. You should acquire some fundamental Italian phrases and vocabulary, as well as some of the local dialects and languages that are peculiar to Cinque Terre.

You should also pick the finest choice for accessing the internet in Cinque Terre, based on your requirements and tastes. You may utilize free Wi-Fi hotspots, purchase a local SIM card with an internet connection, or use your own mobile data plan with roaming costs. By doing so, you may connect with the locals courteously and pleasantly, and access the web information and services that you require. Communication and internet connectivity in Cinque Terre is not only a necessary skill but also a tool to enrich your holiday experience.

Useful Apps and Websites for Cinque Terre

Cinque Terre is a picturesque location on the Italian Riviera, noted for its five colorful towns, spectacular hiking paths, and great food. However, it is also a destination that demands some planning and preparation, since it has significant problems and constraints owing to its topography, popularity, and conservation. Here are some of the best helpful applications and websites for Cinque Terre for 2023-2024, based on ratings, reviews, and popularity.

Cinque Terre is a national park and a UNESCO World Legacy Site that strives to safeguard its natural and cultural legacy. It has various restrictions and regulations that tourists need to obey, such as obtaining a Cinque Terre Card to access the trails, avoiding plastic bags and bottles, and respecting the environment and the residents.

Apps

- **Cinque Terre Hiking Guide:** This app is a must-have for everyone who intends to trek in Cinque

Terre. It contains full maps, descriptions, images, and GPS tracks of all the trails in the region, as well as information on the difficulty, length, elevation, and places of interest of each trip. You may also check the weather forecast, the railway schedule, and the state of the trails in real-time. The app operates offline and is accessible in English, Italian, German, French, and Spanish.

- **Cinque Terre Offline Map:** This program is a basic yet handy tool to traverse Cinque Terre without an internet connection. It includes an offline map of the region that displays the location of the settlements, the railway stations, the trails, the beaches, and other sites of interest. You may also search for locations by name or category, zoom in and out of the map, and receive directions from one area to another. The app is accessible in English.

More Apps and Websites for Cinque Terre

- **Cinque Terre Train:** This software is a helpful tool to schedule your train journeys in Cinque Terre. It gives the train schedule, the ticket costs, the journey time, and the number of stops for each route. You may also check the status of the trains in real-time and receive updates on any delays or cancellations. The app operates offline and is accessible in English, Italian, German, French, and Spanish.

- **Cinque Terre Boat:** This software is a fantastic tool to schedule your boat adventures in Cinque Terre. It includes the boat schedule, the ticket pricing, the trip duration, and the number of stops for each route. You may also check the weather prediction, the sea conditions, and the status of the boats in real-time. The app operates offline and is accessible in English, Italian, German, French, and Spanish.

- **Cinque Terre Hiking:** This website is a complete reference to hiking in Cinque Terre that includes all the information you need to enjoy the trails in the region. It offers information on the difficulty, length, height, and points of interest of each trek, as well as maps, photographs, videos, and reviews. You may also discover recommendations on how to prepare for hiking, what to bring, what to dress, and what to do in case of an emergency. The website is accessible in English.

- **Cinque Terre Insider:** This website is a personal travel blog that gives insider tips and secrets about Cinque Terre. It provides tips on how to avoid tourist traps, how to locate the greatest views, how to enjoy the local culture, how to help the local economy, and how to preserve the environment. It also offers news and updates about Cinque Terre. The website is accessible in English.

- **Cinque Terre Online:** This website is an online booking platform that provides numerous services and goods for Cinque Terre. You can book hotels, apartments, villas, excursions, activities, transfers, car rentals, and more via the website. You may also get information about Cinque Terre's history, culture, food, sights, and events. The website is accessible in English, Italian, German, French, and Spanish.

Cinque Terre is a gorgeous site to visit, but it is also a place that demands some planning and preparation. Luckily, several applications and websites can help you make the most of your vacation there. You can discover information on how to get there, how to move about, where to stay, what to see and do, where to eat and drink, and more. You may also book numerous services and goods online, and receive real-time information on the weather, the trains, the boats, and the trails. Whether you're seeking adventure, leisure, or romance.

CONCLUSION

Cinque Terre is a location that will impress you with its natural and cultural attractions. In this travel guide, we have covered the top sights and activities that you can enjoy in each of the five villages, as well as some of the adjacent towns and cities that are worth a visit. We have also supplied you with some practical information and recommendations on how to organize your vacation, how to get about, where to stay when to travel, and how to keep safe and healthy. We hope that our travel guide will help you make the most of your time in Cinque Terre and have a memorable and pleasurable vacation.

Cinque Terre is a site where you may experience the real and traditional lifestyle of the Ligurian coast, as well as the contemporary and stylish ambiance of the Italian Riviera. You may appreciate the colorful residences, the old churches, the terraced vineyards, and the spectacular sea vistas. You can taste the exquisite fish, the fresh pesto, and the sweet wine. You may trek along the gorgeous paths, kayak along the rocky beach, snorkel in the clear sea, and paraglide over the hills. You may also explore some of the other sites and activities that the area provides, such as Portovenere, Lerici, La Spezia, or Pisa.

Cinque Terre is a destination where you can relax, have fun, and discover something new every day. It is a destination that will fascinate you with its beauty, charm, and variety. It is a spot that you will never forget and that you will want to return to again and again. Cinque Terre is a destination that you will fall in love with.

Printed in Great Britain
by Amazon

28178528R00116